"*Selah* provides excellent nourishment for the soul, or, in Nancie's words, 'food for our faith.' Women will connect at every turn of the page with her spiritual and practical help."

Jill Briscoe, speaker, author of more than forty books,
director of Telling the Truth Ministries Media,
executive editor of *Just between Us* magazine

"What a privilege to take Nancie's book in hand and be mentored chapter by chapter by this incredible, vulnerable, gracious woman of God as she skillfully weaves the Scriptures through our lives. Women so desperately need 'selah' time if they're going to be women of strength and courage prepared for the days which lie before us."

Kay Arthur, CEO and cofounder of
Precept Ministries International

"It's not often that I declare every chapter of a book 'my favorite,' but that is exactly what happened with *Selah*. Each chapter is chock full of material with meaning and relevance to where I have been, where I am, and where I hope to go. *Selah* has its toes dug into the ground while it soars spiritually."

Mary Ann Mayo, certified counselor,
author of twelve books, including
Twilight Travels with Mother

Also by Nancie Carmichael

The Best Things Ever Said about Parenting
The Deeper Life
Desperate for God
Lord, Bless My Child
Lord, Bless This Marriage
601 Quotes about Marriage and Family
Praying for Rain
That Man!
Your Life, God's Home

selah

Your Moment to Stop, Think, and Step into Your Future

NANCIE
CARMICHAEL

Revell
Grand Rapids, Michigan

© 2004 by Nancie Carmichael

Published by Fleming H. Revell
a division of Baker Publishing Group
P.O. Box 6287, Grand Rapids, MI 49516-6287
www.bakerbooks.com

Printed in the United States of America

Library of Congress Cataloging-in-Publication Data
Carmichael, Nancie.
    Selah : your moment to stop, think, and step into your future / Nancie Carmichael.
        p.   cm.
    Includes bibliographical references.
    ISBN 0-8007-5957-5
    1. Christian women—Religious life. 2. Women in the Bible. I. Title
BV4527.C29 2004
248.8′43—dc22   2004004545

When you tear off the layers of everything in a person's life, what remains is faith and family. I am overwhelmed by gratitude to know God's grace and to be surrounded by such a wonderful family—*You are the best!* With all my love I dedicate this book to my husband, Bill, and to my children: to Jon and Brittni, and Willy, Kendsy, and Cali; to Eric and Carly, and "Baby Carm"; to Christian and Jami; to Andrew; and to Amy.

I dedicate this book to the concept that as we submit our lives to God, we will indeed be people that make a difference in our world.

Contents

7

Why Write This Book?
An Introduction

My friend Lily called me one afternoon more than fifteen years ago. I'll never forget that phone call when she asked tearfully, "Nancie, has my life made a difference?"

She was losing her fight with a terminal illness, even though she was too young to die. She had two school-age children and a husband who needed her. I assured her that of course her life had made a difference—to her family, to me, and to many others.

Lily's calling, in addition to caring for her family, was caring for others. As a licensed practical nurse, she had a unique way of helping people recover from surgeries and major illnesses and get on their way to healing. One of her favorite passages of Scripture was from Luke, when Jesus told us, "Consider the lilies, how they grow: they neither toil nor spin; and yet I say to you, even Solomon in all his glory was not arrayed like one of these" (Luke 12:27).

Somehow I think Lily knew that living as God made her was enough. Wouldn't it be for any of us?

And yet . . .

If we're honest, Lily's question is one we all ask. We want our lives to count for something, to make a difference.

Lily died not long after our conversation. I'm thinking more often of her question as I look toward the second half of my life. It seems urgent that I do what's lasting and meaningful.

I too want my life to make a difference.

I know I'm not alone.

I hear from women at a crossroads all the time. Some have realized career goals, raised a family, and already birthed some ministries but now they wonder, *What next?* Some are considering significant change: establishing a new vocation at home or in an office, developing a long-dormant talent, pursuing a new relationship. At the turn of the twentieth century, the average life expectancy for women was forty-eight years. Now it's about eighty-two.[1] We women are living longer and staying fit and active—and we have more expectations. As Dr. Judith Reichman puts it, "We're outliving our ovaries by thirty to thirty-five years. The question is, What do we want to do during that period of time?"[2]

I see my daughter, my daughters-in-law, and my nieces in the first halves of their adult lives. Their world, too, is changing. Now women average about age twenty-five when they marry, and a quarter of all women have not yet had a child before they turn thirty-five, almost double the rate in 1960.[3]

We women have many choices, and the potential for women to make a difference spiritually, economically, morally, socially, and every other way is enormous. Many of us work hard with our families and at our jobs, churches, and our various volunteer work. We are natural-born givers. But at any crossroads—in the pause that God gives us—we have a chance to stop and think. I like to call these pauses "Selah."

When I was a child, my father would read a psalm to my brother and sister and me before we left for school in the morning. "God is our refuge and our strength, a very present help in trouble . . . Selah" (Ps. 46:1, 3 KJV).

"Selah? What does that mean?" I asked.

"It's a pause. It means to stop and think about what you just heard."

I don't know where my father got his facts—maybe from his confirmation classes as a child. I did some digging on the subject, and Dad's definition is probably as good as any. There is no real agreement on what *Selah* means. Some believe it is a musical notation. The New Living Translation uses the word *Interlude:* "The LORD Almighty is here among us; the God of Israel is our fortress. Interlude" (Ps. 46:7 NLT).

There are some who believe that *Selah* comes from the same root as the Hebrew word *Calah*, meaning to weigh, to measure.[4] As in the message written on the wall to Belshazzar: "You have been weighed on the balances and have failed the test" (Dan. 5:27 NLT). So *Selah* could also mean a time to weigh, to evaluate.

As I read through the Psalms and Habakkuk where *Selah* is used, it seems the word is a boundary, a marker. A place to stop and observe, to be still. But regardless of what we call it, we need Selah in our lives—no matter where we are in our journey.

Selah helps us remember who we are; it's a place to be still, to know God. It's a place where we can deal with choices and changes. In these pauses, we're reminded that we have a certain number of days, and we can ask ourselves, Do I want to spend the rest of my life doing what I'm doing? In these places, we see things we need to add or to let go.

I need Selah in my life more than ever, and I suspect you do too. We live in a world of information coming at us. A *lot* of information. Some of it is trivial, some of it important. But we need these pauses in the presence of God to examine our priorities—to pursue what matters most.

Some of us simply need affirmation that we are investing our lives exactly as we should be, that we are answering our calling. Some of us need radical change, an overhaul, or an about-face. Some of us are on the edge of a breathtaking new adventure. And some of us aren't sure what God wants for us, but we're eager to know.

As I talk with women from all walks of life, I'm struck by the fact that each life is an amazing miracle in all its complexity, difficulties, and gifts. I'm awed by some of the women I meet. They aren't couch potatoes! They hike, jog, climb mountains. Many are deeply involved in Bible study and ministry in the church. Some of them have financial means and want to travel. Some have confronted great losses or encountered incredible pain. Some are working to provide a living. Some are courageously dealing with difficult and chronic circumstances.

Regardless of their situations, they seem to share a universal quest to spend the next part of life wisely in order to know what my friend Lily longed to understand: Has my life made a difference?

Come Join the Conversation

I have written this book because it's often through conversations with other women that we learn about ourselves. I hope you will see this book as a conversation with me and with others as we explore stories of people in the Bible and in contemporary times. (I did use my imagination and took some liberties in developing some of the Bible stories, trying to feel what it was really like for those people thousands of years ago.) Stories are important to us women. We listen to speakers at events and see our own stories in theirs. We love epic romances and dramas.

I remember my mother having friends over for coffee, and I loved to hang around, listening to their conversation. Sometimes, when the conversation got really interesting, my mother sent me out of the room on some trumped-up excuse—and I knew I was missing some great details.

We women do lunch or coffee differently than men. It's the details, the stories, that grip us. In our Bible study groups and book clubs, we examine stories of people in the Word and learn from them. We share our own. In that way, we grapple with the issue of meaning and purpose for our lives. Each of our lives is like a story being written, and we are active participants in the process.

My vision for this book is that as you read it, you will think about the story of your own amazing and unique life. It will be even better if you can share this book in a circle of a few friends or in a book club or Bible study setting. We learn so much from each other, no matter where we are in our journey.

At the Crossroads

A crossroads is a pivotal place. We choose to embrace it or live in the past. From my own place of the empty nest, I am realizing what a challenging, yet wonderful place this is. In midlife, the years ahead can look intimidating. But the good news is that it can be the most productive and satisfying time of life. A 1998 Gallup survey showed that more than half of American women between the ages of fifty and sixty-five felt happiest and most fulfilled than at any other stage of life.[5]

Dare to Answer the Call

Another reason I wrote this book is to reassure women wherever they are that the best is yet to be. If you are in the first half of your adult life, open your eyes to the Selahs in your life so that you can embrace your life with all that you have and are. If you are in the second half of your adult life, take time to understand and appreciate the gift of your life. If you already know your purpose, it's time now to give it fresh vision and new energy. If you are not yet aware of your purpose, I hope this book will help you understand what it is.

I loved the process of interviewing and hearing responses from more than thirty women on this subject. We had lunch. We had coffee. We talked! We laughed and cried. The women I talked to represented many occupations, life experiences, and ages. But their common thread was their love for God and their passion to make a difference in their worlds. Their worlds varied: Several worked at churches; two were artists. I interviewed a missionary, pastors' wives, professional women, women in community leadership, a nurse, a schoolteacher, a rancher's wife, and women caring for their families. They were the busiest women I knew! Some of them e-mailed me their responses from wherever they were in the world. One breathlessly dropped her form by the house, in a hurry to reach her son's soccer game.

Another common thread in their responses told me that knowing one's calling and answering it means almost more than life itself. Each stage of life has its vulnerabilities and joy. The first half of your adult life (which I deal with in part 1 and call First Calling) is a time in our lives so full we can hardly think; it is a time that has to be productive with work, developing friendships and family, and caring for everything that goes along with that. In this half of life, we receive good things—rich experiences as well as pain, loss, and disappointment.

Then there is a pause when transition begins to happen—a Selah (part 2) where it's important to take time to see where we are. A drastic event may signal a change.

Perhaps our children begin leaving home. Our bodies change. There can be the death of a spouse, or a shattering divorce. Perhaps we sense a stirring to go back to school, change careers, start a new relationship, or pursue new hobbies. This is a time, I believe, when it's important to take time to embrace what God is putting before us, because we can lose hope if we keep trying to generate energy and purpose from something that worked in the past.

As hope fizzles, so do our dreams. In some ways, this time of life is like adolescence—there may be some floundering. If you're like me, it can be hard to stop, to be still. To wait. We are tempted to fill these places with business as usual or meaningless activity. But these pauses can be significant and life shaping if we pay attention to them. In them, we have the opportunity to confront changes and choices we must make, responsibilities we must assume, things we must let go.

In a way, it is like a Sabbath—from which we get the word *sabbatical*. How great it would be if we women could take sabbaticals at this crucial place in life! And we can, in some ways, if we are intentional about it.

Then we come to what I call the Second Calling (part 3). We come to this place in life full of experiences, where we give out of what we have been given. It is a fruitful place. What we have by this time is wisdom, humility, and an awareness of our gifts as well as shortcomings. And, hopefully, a well-developed sense of humor!

So come along with me on this adventure as you take a well-deserved break to see what you have been given, where you are now, and how to go from here to live a life that makes a difference.

As the songwriter says:

> When it's all been said and done;
> There is just one thing that matters:

15

Did I do my best to live for Truth?
Did I live my life for You?

When all's been said and done;
All my treasures will mean nothing;
Only what I've done for love's reward
Will stand the test of time.[6]

PART 1

Your First Calling

The First Calling is a time of gathering. Think of yourself making a quilt: You gather the pieces of fabric you will use . . . lots of pieces, all colors and kinds. It takes some people years to collect all the bits they need. The designs are unique—some have contrasting colors of light and dark, and some have more subtle shadings. Some of the designs are traditional, handed down from generations, even though they may have a unique twist. Some are more abstract and contemporary.

Either way, the quilt is an expression of the one who made it.

And your one-of-a-kind life is an expression of you. Through the material you have been given, through your choices, you have the potential to make something wonderful.

1

Saying Yes

The Woman at the Well:
Available and Willing

> The only thing I can give to God is "my right to
> myself." If I will give God that, He will make a holy
> experiment out of me, and God's experiments always
> succeed.
>
> Oswald Chambers, *Our Brilliant Heritage*

The woman had seen a lot of life. But even with all her
life experiences, she still had the unfortunate knack
for picking the wrong man—again and again! How many
romances had failed? Five marriages so far, and too many
other relationships to count. She didn't even keep track
of those. She knew the village folk didn't accept her life-
style, but she'd given up trying to live up to other people's
standards. A deep need for love and acceptance drove her
from man to man.

She usually went to the well for water in the afternoon,
when all the other women weren't around. They could

be cruel—the silences, the looks, the whispers. She knew what they were saying. As much as she craved and needed real friends, she was definitely outside the circle. She knew she'd better just try to make the best of it.

Alone at night and early mornings, she had moments when she felt despair for the emptiness of her life. What was it all for? She knew that men used her, but at least they showed her some acceptance. As the years and relationships accumulated, her youth faded and her body attracted men less. The harder she tried, the emptier life became, and the future seemed hopeless.

Then there was that ordinary, amazing day when everything in her life turned upside down. As was her habit, she went to the well outside the city to get water when no one else was there. A man was sitting by the well, a Jewish man. She could tell from his dress and appearance. He looked tired and dusty. He startled her when he spoke to ask her for a drink of water. Jews just didn't deal with the Samaritans—not to mention the fact that she was a woman, and alone in the afternoon at the well. Her thoughts raced. Was he coming on to her or what?

Thus began an astonishing conversation. He told her that if she knew who he was, she would have asked *him* for water . . . "living water" at that. That was an intriguing thought. Living water? Yes, he said. It was water so satisfying that she would never want for anything else, and it would become a perpetual spring within her, giving her eternal life.

Impulsively, she said yes. That's what she wanted, needed. Jesus told her to go get her husband to continue the conversation, and then she had to admit the truth. She didn't—at the time—have a husband. And Jesus, with a penetrating, loving look, said, "You're right! You don't have a husband—for you have had five husbands, and you aren't even married to the man you're living with now" (John 4:17–18 NLT).

She tried to change the subject, to get more philosophical. She suddenly realized she was not talking to an ordinary man. This man could search her mind and see inside her life—inside her very soul! Let's talk religion, she suggested, how people worship . . . denominational differences.

But Jesus kept coming back to the heart issue and told her that "true worshipers will worship the Father in spirit and in truth. The Father is looking for anyone who will worship him that way. For God is Spirit, so those who worship him must worship in spirit and in truth" (John 4:23–24 NLT).

She knew there was a Messiah who was going to come—the one who would be called Christ. She knew about that way-off hope. Someday the Messiah would have the answer, and he would solve everything. Then Jesus told her, "I am the Messiah!" And she believed. How could she not? He knew things about her no one else did. His words were like water to a dying soul, and she took them in, no holds barred. No tentative steps of faith here; she plunged in all the way. For the first time she had hope, a future. The Messiah—talking to *her,* offering "living water" to *her!* She grabbed on to the truth and was so excited she left her water jar by the well and ran back to the village to tell everyone she saw.

Her newfound faith was so contagious, people followed her from the village out to hear Jesus, and Scripture records that many of the Samaritans heard the message and believed that Jesus was the Savior of the world.

What We Can Learn from the Woman at the Well

Say Yes

C. S. Lewis said, "There are only two kinds of people in the end: Those who say to God, 'Thy will be done,' and those to whom God says, 'Okay, go ahead and have it your way.'"[1] Scripture doesn't tell us how the woman's life developed, but what was pivotal in her life was making the most important choice anyone can—to say yes to the living water of Jesus.

Saying yes to God is the beginning place of real life for every one of us. For me, it occurred when I was a very young child, after hearing the story of the cross; and then later as a college freshman, I reaffirmed that yes in a deserted chapel late at night.

Depending upon who and where we are, we come to faith in Christ in different ways. Vonette Bright says that although she grew up in the church, God was not a reality in her life. As a young woman, she met Bill Bright. They had a whirlwind romance but waited three years to be married.

During that time, Bill was growing in his faith, and Vonette was getting farther away from hers, deciding he had become a religious fanatic.

Around that time, and through Bill, Vonette met Dr. Henrietta Mears, director of Christian education at Holly-wood Presbyterian Church. "Since I minored in chemistry in college, it made sense to me to add the person of Jesus Christ to the ingredients of faith I already knew. I received Jesus Christ as my personal Savior. As a result, God has become a vital reality in my life, giving me identity and direction."[2]

Vonette and Bill Bright went on to have an amazing career as they established Campus Crusade for Christ, and they have influenced thousands to come to know Jesus. But all Vonette knew—and all any of us know when we say yes—is that we need something deeper, something of substance that will complete our identity and shape us through the years.

Like the woman at the well, we know there's something more to life than the obvious, and when we are presented with the truth and see it, we say yes!

Say Yes in Each Season

Love bade me welcome; yet my soul drew back, guilty of
dust and sin.
But quick-eyed love, observing me grow slack from my
first entrance in,
Drew nearer to me, sweetly questioning if I lack'd anything.

George Herbert

Look at your life. Where are you now, and how can you
say yes to God from where you are? Life is constantly
changing. You may be very young, just getting started in
your journey, wanting to know what's ahead. You may be
a mother with children still at home, and from watching
your children grow, you realize you are in an entirely different place now from where you were even five years ago.
You may be considering a change of jobs, maybe an entirely
different occupation. You may have lost your mate; suddenly your whole paradigm has changed, and you are in a
place you never wanted to be—but here you are. Perhaps
your children are grown and life is suddenly strange; you're
wondering where you fit now.

Sometimes in life we feel very much like the woman at
the well—we need a refreshing drink of Living Water in the
middle of our journey. It reminds me of the story of Jacob,
when he ran away from home under bad circumstances
(see Gen. 28:10–22). In the middle of the night as he slept
with a rock for a pillow, he dreamed of angels ascending
and descending. He awoke exclaiming, "Surely the LORD
is in this place, and I did not know it. . . . How awesome
God is in this place!" (28:16–17).

It's often the place where we feel most uncertain and
afraid where we can open our eyes to see that he *is* present and he is awesome. In all of the changes of life, he
is unchanging. His love is constant, never ending, never

23

failing. Romans asks, "Who shall separate us from the love of Christ? . . . Neither height nor depth, nor anything else in all creation, will be able to separate us from the love of God" (Rom. 8:35, 39 NIV).

What brings Living Water to our souls is believing who he is: the Christ, the Son of God. Saying yes to him changes us as we trust and follow him from wherever we are.

Nancy, wife of a rancher and mother of five in Montana, tells me that she said yes to Christ as a young woman. She says, "What it means to be a servant of Christ keeps changing. I now have two of my children in college, two in high school, and one in junior high. I'm helping to care for my elderly aunts and my mother as well as support my husband and be active and available in running our ranch. What's in the future for me? Time will tell. I just want to be used of God and to be faithful."

Say Yes from Who You Are

It's comforting to realize that God calls us from who and what we are. You hear the call and present who you are—not who you wish you were—to see what he will make of you. That is how to answer the First Calling on your life. Saying yes to him is saying you recognize that he knows what's best for you and you are available for him to use.

That's when the stories of our lives with God begin and develop. Together with him, we build our lives the way we build a quilt: piece by piece, using various colors, light and dark, and creating contrasts. Putting together a quilt may take years of gathering material before we even know what the pieces are going to be, how it will look. But initially we must decide that we *are* going to make a quilt! As we stay patiently committed to the creative process, we see that it is becoming beautiful, that it is *for* something, and that all those pieces we weren't sure were worth anything are finally making sense in the overall picture.

Getting to that place takes time. If you're like me, sometimes you feel bogged down in the seemingly meaningless
details, wondering what on earth all the fractured pieces are
for: *What good am I doing, and is this what I wanted so many
years ago?* I believe that saying yes to God is to accept his
love and grace for us and to give him our worship.

Warren Wiersbe says it well: "We are either fashioning our
lives by pressure from without, or we are transforming our
lives by power from within. The difference is worship."[3]

> The coming of Christ into our lives is an issue of surrender
> and opening our lives. Our many quarreling selves become
> one in salvation. . . . Only when Christ comes in do we dis-
> cover our own definition and why we are in the world. . . .
> We are saved from living the undefined life.
>
> Calvin Miller, *Walking with the Saints*[4]

The story of how the prophet Samuel became a mighty
force in the time of Israel, when "the word of the LORD
was rare," is an intriguing one (1 Sam. 3:1 NIV). He was a
gift from God to his mother, who at first seemed unable to
have children. Overjoyed at his birth, she promised him
to God and brought him to the temple at a young age to
minister to the priest Eli.

The birth of every child is ripe with promise. The births
of each of our four sons and the adoption of our daughter
were amazing, never-to-be-forgotten moments for Bill and
me as we thought in wonder, *Here is a new life, with a unique
calling and personality.* Samuel certainly had a unique calling ahead of him, as he later became deeply influential in
his nation.

One night when Samuel was still a young boy, God called
him: "Samuel!" At first he thought Eli needed him and
ran to his side. After Samuel had been awakened several
times, Eli realized God was calling the boy, and he told him,
"Next time you hear your name being called, answer, 'Lord,

here am I; your servant hears.'" And Samuel answered yes to the call.

As a young man, Isaiah was moved by the presence of God, and when God asked, "Who will go for Me? Whom can I send?" Isaiah responded in complete humility, "Here I am. Send me!" *Here I am.* Not "Here is what I think you need," or "Here is what I will try to be." It's: "Here I am. Such as I am. Such as you created me, I am available for your purposes."

Saying yes to God from who we are is the best decision we will ever make. And while there is that initial decision to follow Christ, it seems to me that in each phase of our lives, we can continue to say yes to him as we grow and change.

My mother would say, "Bloom where you are planted," which may seem like a cliché, but it's a great principle. The woman at the well went back to where she was from—her village—and shared what she had learned. She didn't move away to another region to tell her good news, but she began where she was, with people she knew.

Early Passions Shape Your Call

> O earth, you're too wonderful for anybody to realize you. . . .
> Do any human beings ever realize life while they have
> it?—every, every minute?
>
> Thornton Wilder, *Our Town*

Think back to when you were ten or twelve years old. What were your hopes and dreams? What did you love to do more than anything? What made you *you*?

I'm one of seven children raised on a farm, and I grew up with a sense of adventure. Our parents gave me and my siblings a lot of freedom to play outside. We sometimes took eggs from the henhouse or dug potatoes from the garden. Then we hiked out to a grove of trees, where we camped

26

for most of the day and pretended, played, and explored. When we got hungry, we scrambled the eggs in a pan over a campfire or roasted the potatoes in the coals. I loved being outdoors. There was something so vital about it—feeling the wind on my face, hearing the meadowlarks, standing under the huge expanse of sky.

I attended a little country schoolhouse across the street from where we lived (half of the twelve or so students were my brothers and sisters). We had an unusual and wonderful teacher who taught us to memorize poetry and love good books. Since we had no television at home, the highlight of our week was going into town on Saturday and getting another stack of books to read from the library. My oldest sister was a writer and encouraged me in my writing. We also loved music. Piano lessons were very important—memorizing a good piece, getting the phrasing just so.

These were early callings that I just seemed to adopt naturally. It was not work; it was simply the way my life developed—along with my parents' love of God and involvement in the local church. These things shaped me. There was also the dream to find the right man, to marry, have children, build a life. My sisters and I converted an old woodshed to a playhouse in which we put our dolls and playthings. When our brothers could take charge of the shed, they converted it into a fort from which they shot imaginary enemies. (That was my earliest lesson on the differences between men and women and the power struggles that exist. Let there be no mistake—we are different!)

The point is, our early passions and dreams help shape who we become as adults. I am grateful for my childhood and feel I have been given much. I've had pain and disappointment too, but I feel so blessed by what I've received. My parents' early lives were marked by loss and betrayal and deprivation. Yet they came to Christ in their twenties, and they nourished us with their faith.

My daughter spent her first three and a half years in a poor orphanage in Korea, and although she has blossomed and developed, those early years still shape some of her thinking and her self-concept. We try to encourage her with this truth from Dr. Richard Dobbins: "It's not so much the story of your life as what you tell yourself about the story of your life."[5]

Even now, my family and home are great passions. I still love music and good books. My beloved grand piano is up here in my writing loft. I've been married to a great man of principle and faith and love, and I'm privileged to be a mother to five wonderful children and grandmother to three (so far!). Laurie Beth Jones writes, "We live according to the words which have been declared for us, either consciously or unconsciously. Words are prophecies which pull us, shape us, guide us."[6]

As you look back on your childhood, what early influences and passions (or perhaps prophecies and visions from significant people in your life) helped shape you? What words pulled and guided you?

Know Who You Are

When we are young, we make important choices that help determine the pattern of our lives: where we go to school, whom we marry (if we do marry), where we live, what our work will be. So we get to a certain place in life, and our stories seem to have a specific shape. Our lives are well ordered, or maybe unconventional. (Yes, there are crazy quilts!) We live with the design we have helped to create—a job, a career, children. And then things change. For a while. But the story isn't finished.

Maybe the job situation shifts. The family structure alters. The inevitability of loss hits you. Or you experience a deep disappointment, and you see that life is not turning out the way you thought it would. Still, we have the nagging sense that somehow there is something more, that we were created for something bigger, something that fits. We have a yearning to know and live out our calling, to rediscover the first love and passion of our lives.

It's important to understand and appreciate who you are. As Os Guinness writes, "Recognizing who we aren't is only the first step toward knowing who we are."[7] Sometimes we think that saying yes to God and living out the calling he has for us means we are supposed to go somewhere, do something specific (especially if we don't want to), such as be a missionary overseas. A retired missionary told me, "I'm glad I got to go to the mission field. The best years of my life were spent there. The exhilaration of sharing the gospel in new places with new people can't even be described. It was such an adventure, and we did it as a family." One of the sure signs she was supposed to be a missionary in the Far East was her joy and sense of fulfillment.

We are all called to various things, and how great to know that we can trust him with our lives; that joy marks our callings. Christ doesn't call us to an occupation—a series of accomplishments, an impressive résumé, or a statement of net worth. Christ calls us to himself. And there is joy in saying yes to him—it's not drudgery. A worship chorus expresses this: "Jesus . . . all for Jesus. All I am, and have and ever hope to be."

Who Influenced You?

Yesterday was a beautiful, sunny Sunday afternoon. I'd been working on this book for a while and needed a break. I asked my husband, "Bill, do you want to walk along the Metolius River with me?" He looked up from his paper and said, "Sure!" We're convinced we live close to one of the most beautiful places on earth—a sparkling river that flows from deep below the earth out of a spring less than a mile from here. We visit it often. It's lined by massive ponderosa pine trees, willows, and an amazing variety of wildflowers. As I walked the trail and savored the sound and sight of the rushing river, I became aware of how overwhelmed I was feeling with trying to finish this book with the message that I know God had impressed on me to share. I simply prayed, "Holy Spirit, I need you."

Although it's an early spring, and a cold one, I was hoping we would see some wildflowers blooming. We did! I counted them—eight different varieties. Tiny white flowers, purple ones. Suddenly Bill said, "Look! A yellow warbler." A small, exquisite yellow bird with a hint of pale green was nesting in a spot near the water in a willow tree. Later we went home, refreshed. That evening I read from Oswald Chambers's devotional, My Utmost for His Highest. The entry for that day:

> Consider the lilies of the field, how they grow, they simply are! Think of the sea, the air, the sun, the stars and the moon—all these are, and what a ministration they exert. So often we mar God's designed influence through us by our self-conscious effort to be consistent and useful. Jesus says that there is only one way to develop spiritually, and that is by concentration on God. "Do not bother about being of use to others; believe on Me"—pay attention to the Source, and out of you will flow rivers of living water. We cannot get at the springs of our natural life by common sense, and Jesus is teaching that growth in spiritual life does not depend on our watching it, but on concentration on our Father in heaven. Our heavenly Father knows the circumstances we are in, and if we keep concentrated on Him we will grow spiritually as the lilies.
>
> The people who influence us most are not those who buttonhole us and talk to us, but those who live their lives

like the stars in heaven and the lilies in the field, perfectly simply and unaffectedly. Those are the lives that mold us.

If you want to be of use to God, get rightly related to Jesus Christ and He will make you of use unconsciously every minute you live.[8]

Christine, an artist and mother of three, who just celebrated her fiftieth birthday in Hawaii with her husband, told me, "The biggest change in my life from twenty years ago is that my purpose is now *being* instead of *doing*."

Think about it: Who are the people who made a difference in your life, the people who most deeply influenced you? Most likely, if they are like the people who have most influenced me, they were not celebrities—they were just ordinary folk. My mother and father, who are both gone now, lived their lives, honest struggles and all, in the crucible of family life, being true and faithful, reading the Bible, supporting the local church, loving us children. Yes, they often worried and felt inadequate. In spite of that, Jesus shone through their lives, and besides, they were fun to live with!

Other important influences include my piano teacher, Mrs. Bain, who taught me to love good music, and week after week, year after year, she helped me make music out of stumbling attempts. Dorothy and Earl Book, who were our pastors when Bill and I were youth pastors, showed us how to love Jesus by loving people. Grandma Ferlen, an eighty-nine-year-old woman in the church, showed me how to pray and to believe God when it seemed impossible. My husband's parents show us even now how to live a life of prayer and faithful love for family and friends. My husband and children, my close friends, and my prayer group all show me that it is possible to make a difference simply by saying yes from who I am.

<hr>

Prayer

Lord, like the woman at the well, we say yes to your living water, realizing that real purpose and direction in life begin with knowing you. And we reaffirm that yes, knowing that our lives are a work in progress, and that we are your workmanship. Develop us as you will. May our hearts and minds be open to whatever you have for us, knowing that your ways are perfect and we can trust you. In Christ's name, amen.

Mapping Your Next Step

Read John 4:1–42.

- After the woman at the well had her encounter with the Messiah, were there any noticeable differences in her demeanor and behavior? What were they?
- Discuss what you think it means to say yes to God. What practical difference does it make in your life?
- What new situation are you facing? What are you learning about God and yourself in this new place?

How wonderful that he calls us from who and what we are! Here are some discussion questions to help you understand who you are and what your passions might be:

- Think back to when you were twelve years old. What did you dream of becoming then?
- Where and when do you really come alive?
- What project have you been so involved in that you lose track of time?

2

What's My Message?

The Proverbs 31 Woman:
Developing the Message

Live your life while you have it. Life is a splendid gift.
There is nothing small in it. For the greatest things
grow by God's law out of the smallest. But to live your
life you must discipline it. You must not fritter it away
. . . but make your thoughts, your acts, all work to the
same end and that end, not self but God. That is what
we call character.

Florence Nightingale

The woman was incredible. Organized, ambitious—every-thing she touched became successful, and she was mar-ried to an outstanding man in the community. Her husband
and children adored her. Her beautiful home showed her
creative flair. Not only that, she was an absolute knockout
for a woman her age and dressed in the most stylish clothes.
Neighbors whispered that she made them herself. What's
more, she sewed for her own children—and they actually
liked and wore the outfits she made! You would hate her,

except for the fact that she was the nicest person you could ever meet. Nobody could recall an unkind word from her mouth.

She was kind, gracious, and talented. It's true that she was all of those, but another outstanding quality she possessed was helping people who were down-and-out. She wasn't afraid to get her hands dirty. The more you got to know her, you began to realize her secret: She loved God with her whole self, and everything she did and said radiated from her very lively relationship with him. And while you admired her gifts, it was her faith in God that was so contagious, and you wanted to know her God so that his strength could be yours too.

What a woman! The description of the Proverbs 31 standard has given all of us Christian women a bit of a struggle, if we're honest. Who can live up to all of these things? It's comforting to know that she wasn't real—she was an ideal. King Lemuel's mother described this wonderful woman to her son and said, in so many words, "Pick out this kind of wife!" No wonder she exclaimed, "The virtuous woman—who can find her? She's as rare and highly prized as a precious jewel." For sure! Trying to emulate her example can be daunting—unless we remember that the sum of it all is verse 30: "A woman who fears the LORD, she shall be praised." That's the heart of her message, shown by how she lived.

What We Can Learn from the Proverbs 31 Woman

Contemplate Your Life Message

What do you think people will praise you for someday? What is your life message? Walk through any graveyard, and notice some of the epitaphs on the stones—the story of a life described in a sentence or two. Sometimes it's a good exercise to wonder what the message of your life would be if it were distilled to a few sentences, or even paragraphs. There's the story of the woman who had been something of a hypochondriac and wanted as her epitaph "I told you I was sick!" As I thought about mine, I decided maybe it would be "Most days, I did the best I could. (Then there were those others when I just wanted to eat a Snickers bar and read a magazine!)"

But the message of our lives is not as simple as a sentence or two. We experience a mixture of good times and hard times, triumphs and tragedies. We do have our phases. And yet how we live each day builds the ultimate message of our lives. The little things, the daily choices we make, help us become who we are.

It's like the poem we learned as children:

> Little drops of water,
> Little grains of sand
> Make the mighty ocean and the pleasant land.
> Thus the little minutes, humble tho' they be—
> Make the mighty ages of eternity.[1]

Be Kind

The description of the Proverbs 31 woman is beautifully told in an acrostic, which is actually poetry. Her example still instructs women thousands of years later. The small acts of compassion, the creativity, the serving, the kind words—all describe a great woman with a great message. Verse 26 reveals her as a woman of wisdom, and that on "her tongue is the law of kindness."

What a simple yet profound thing it is to be kind. Henry Drummond wrote in 1884, "The greatest thing a man can do for his Heavenly Father is to be kind to some of His other children. I wonder why it is that we are not all kinder than we are? How much the world needs it! How easily it is done! How instantaneously it acts! How infallibly it is remembered!"[2]

Find Your Passion—Find Your Message

If she were alive today, no doubt the Proverbs 31 woman who quilted her own bedspreads would want to come to central Oregon in July, because we hold the ultimate quilt show. Although I don't quilt, I love to look at them because they tell stories. It has become quite an American art form.

I accuse my friends who quilt of belonging to a cult, because they are so passionate about it! Every July more than twenty thousand women descend on our little town of Sisters (population 1,081) for the annual quilt show Jean Wells started in 1979. Women come to take quilting classes, display their quilts, or just walk around town to appreciate the beautiful and unique designs that hang from every building. The quilts are like art, each an expression of the person who created it, and each one carries a distinct message.

Quilts can be a metaphor for our lives. One woman said she "sewed the patches of her life—the light and the dark all make up the complex patchwork of a lifetime." Another woman, Freddy, explained her passion for quilting: "I want to leave a heritage for my grandchildren. I want them to know that I walked through this life and that I contributed . . . that I made a little corner of the world more beautiful." Each of us is in the process of "quilting" her own bedspread, developing her own life story that is her life's message.

We develop our message by the way we live, by what becomes important to us: how we spend our money, what makes us laugh, what we read, the movies and television programs we watch, what we feed our souls and spirits and minds and bodies, and what we say to others about others. Ordinary day after ordinary day, we develop our message. There are dark places in all our lives, but they add depth and beauty to the overall picture.

What seems to help the ultimate shape of our message is our passion—*what we love*. How satisfying it is when we can grab hold of a sense of our calling to live a focused life, a life with purpose and goals. A life with a clear message. Proverbs 31:28 says, "Her children arise and call her blessed" (NIV). When my children were small, I used to say, "My children don't rise up and call me 'blessed.' They just rise up and call me!" Again, though, the heart of the Proverbs 31 woman is in verse 30: "A woman who fears the LORD, she shall be praised"! Out of that passion for God, her life had its definition and message.

Don't Forgo Form for Substance

There is a provocative story within a story in 2 Samuel 18:19–33. It tells of Ahimaaz and how much he wanted to carry a message. Ahimaaz was the son of Zadok the priest at a tragic time of King David's reign—when his son Absalom was trying to steal the hearts of the people from his father and take over the throne. David loved his son desperately, but he still had to defend his throne. David was away from the battle while his general Joab was trying to put down the rebellion. Absalom, riding under the branches of a terebinth tree, got his long hair tangled in the branches and was caught—he became a perfect target. Joab thrust three spears into Absalom's body, and the handsome, rebellious son of David died.

The battle scene had to be chaotic, with the war ending along with Absalom's death. A lot of soldiers were milling about, and Ahimaaz wanted to run to David with the message. (Since those were the days before CNN, runners delivered the news!) The official messenger was a Cushite—an Ethiopian. But Ahimaaz loved to run. He was eager, and no doubt he had developed good timing. He had great form, and maybe he was like Eric Liddell, the famous Olympian who said he sensed God's smile when he ran. The Cushite left with the message for David, but Ahimaaz begged Joab, "Let me run."

Finally Joab said, "Go," probably just to get him out of there. And Ahimaaz ran. He ran so well and so fast, he beat the Cushite and arrived at the city gates where David was waiting to hear news of the battle. Ahimaaz bowed before David and told him, "Blessed be the LORD your God, who has delivered up the men who raised their hand against my lord the king!" (2 Sam. 18:28). But David wanted to know about his son: Was Absalom safe?

To his chagrin, Ahimaaz realized he couldn't tell King David what he wanted most to hear. He'd outrun the Cushite—but he was not able to deliver the message. And David said to him, "Stand aside!" Surely this was an embarrassment for him—his big moment before the king, and he said nothing. All his great running added up to a big zero. Finally the official message carrier, the Cushite, arrived and gave David the devastating message.

It's easy to spend so much time on form that we forget substance. We run . . . run . . . run . . . and we may look good, but what is our message? Do we even have a message? Or are we just busy? M. Craig Barnes, pastor of the National Presbyterian Church in Washington, D.C., writes,

> We keep jam-packed Daytimers close to our side as if they are the modern equivalent of the six shooter from the old cowboy movies. They make us feel powerful, and if anyone asks for an appointment, we whip out those weapons and say, "Well, I don't know. Let's see if I have any free time. When? Oh no, I couldn't possibly do it then." We even like to look busy. Who wants to hear from someone, "You look well rested." No, what we want to hear is, "Say, you look tired. You must be really busy." Busy is good. It means we are running hard. It means we are doing all we can to find a blessing before someone sounds the buzzer and life is over.[3]

Ouch. That hits me where it hurts. Years ago, when Bill was on the staff of a church and our children were small, my neighbor said wistfully to me one day, "You're always dressed up, and you're always going to church." I wanted to say, "So? Is there a problem with that, lady? This is good, you know." It wasn't until years later that I realized the message my frenetic life was sending to her: "I'm a busy, busy Christian woman—too busy to talk to you, neighbor! Or to listen."

When I think back to the days of mothering five active children, trying to keep up with a busy husband who was involved in many things (often getting me involved along with him), participating in and chauffeuring to church activities, school, sports, and programs—life just came at me then, and it was difficult to have quiet moments. Difficult but not impossible. How important it is to establish boundaries that can help protect and feed us in order for us to develop the heart of our message.

Choose What's Best

It's possible to be victims of our own success—to run so well and so fast the message gets lost. Or maybe it never really develops as it could, into substance. Many things drive us. In the questionnaires and surveys I sent out to various women, I heard from them repeatedly: If they had it to do over again, they would spend less time worrying about what other people think. One woman, Nita, said she "got too caught up in the details trying to please some invisible audience." Judy, a former pastor's wife and mother of three children and four stepchildren, said, "I did these senseless, ingrown church activities that took enormous amounts of energy and time but had no real long-term effect. Now I am involved in teaching Sunday school, but my main focus is being involved in community education, and I find this is truly my calling."

We find ourselves doing many things because of our work or our children. Our involvement in school and church and community can drive us with the tyranny of the urgent. They are good involvements, though, and I am awed at how much women do to keep the schools, communities, and churches going.

It's easy to become fragmented, even as we fill our lives with good things. Jim Collins writes, "Good is the enemy of great." Collins and his team researched what made the difference between great and good companies. He found that the companies that rose above the standard were led by people who were committed to the concepts and mission statements of their companies. His contention is that the great leaders were more consumed by what they were building, creating, and contributing rather than what they got—fame, fortune, adulation, or power.[4]

I think that principle can apply to us as individuals too. To say yes to many things, even good things—if it doesn't fit the message of your life—is to say no to the best. But how much more powerful and effective is our giving when it comes from a core message instead of just a to-do list.

One woman said (and many others echoed her), "My mind is always on the next task, and I find it hard to live in the moment."

Sharon, a wife and mother, said, "Why is it that it seems so much of my life is spent on tasks, not people—when it's people I really want to spend time on?"

John Ortberg writes of this tension from an experience he had one night as he was bathing and drying his daughter. As three-year-olds can do, she was dancing around, and he was trying to get the job done, so he said, "Stop with the dee dah day stuff and get over here!"

She asked simply, "Why?" and he realized he had no good answer, so he got up and danced with her.

He says,

Reflecting on this afterward, I realized that I tend to divide my minutes into two categories: living, and waiting to live. Most of my life is spent in transit: trying to get somewhere, waiting to begin, driving someplace, standing in line, waiting for a meeting to end, trying to get a task completed, worrying about something bad that might happen, or being angry about something that did not happen. These are all moments when I am not likely to be fully present, not to be aware of the voice and purpose of God. I am impatient. I am, almost literally, killing time. And that is just another way of saying I am killing myself.[5]

I can relate to that. One summer morning, I was trying to get ready for a women's luncheon at the church where my husband was the pastor. I was young—still not thirty years old—but as the pastor's wife, I was the leader of this thing, even though I had three little boys ages six and younger. The previous pastor's wife was gifted in hospitality and had put on a monthly luncheon that was well attended and well received. I assumed (because I thought others expected it of me) that I should try to step into her shoes and pick up where she left off. It didn't occur to me that her children were grown, and she was in an entirely different place in life from where I was then.

I had a defining moment as I stood in the church kitchen, pineapple juice up to my elbows, trying to fashion one hundred pineapple boats into one hundred servings of fruit salad, with three little boys at my feet who were not happy about being in the church kitchen that morning. I wasn't happy being there either. The pineapples were a bit too ripe, and juice was running all over; I realized at that very moment this was not part of the message of my life, no matter what was expected of me!

Instead, I began a Bible study with two other women who wanted one. I absolutely came alive as I saw how much I loved leading the Bible study. Our group started small but soon flourished, and I realized for the first time that teaching was one of my gifts. The previous pastor's wife had the gift of administration—I didn't.

What a relief to know that God didn't create us to be miserable or to be square pegs in round holes. He created each of us differently, with different callings and abilities. As we say yes to him, a unique message that he develops within us emerges, and out of it we share with others.

I enjoy seeing younger women discovering their gifts as their lives unfold. My daughter-in law Brittni (Jon's wife) is a wonderful mother to our three grandchildren, but she is also influential in coaching high school girls. She comes alive on the soccer field as it's obvious that the girls on the team love her and she is a great mentor to them as well as a coach.

Carly, Eric's wife, is gifted with executive skills as well as compassion for those less fortunate. I see her come alive as she deals with concepts of marketing and public relations. My newest daughter-in-law, Chris's wife, Jami, has a passion for history and is doing her graduate work with an eye for teaching. I can imagine her someday infecting her students with her love of history. My daughter, Amy, is working right now in an assisted living facility with the elderly and is realizing she loves older people.

Another young woman I know, Michelle, recently made a courageous change in location and college in order to pursue her passion for nursing.

Shape Your Unique Message

Shaping our own unique message is a process of discovery, of trying different things, of learning where we come alive, of seeing what is our passion. And then it is a matter of saying no to things that are not part of our message. It's a process of letting Jesus have more and more of that talent and ability as he develops us. But to do that, it's important to find quiet moments—Selahs—in order to stop and think.

This is hard for us women, because we tend to take care of the whole world before we take care of ourselves. But if Jesus, God's Son, needed to go away frequently to quiet times to talk to his Father, how much more do we need it? In order for us to have a message, and not be hollow at the core, we must be sure that we get nourished ourselves. It takes time and discipline. It takes personal study of God's Word and periodic evaluation of our commitments and priorities. How do we find those quiet moments in our crazy lives? We must go out of our way and be creative about making this time a priority.

At this very moment, I am sitting on the deck of a friend's house, which overlooks a beautiful lake. She knew my need to get away, and since she was going to be gone a few days, she told me to use her home. I gratefully accepted. My own house can distract me, even when I'm alone. I see furniture that needs dusting, floors that need to be swept, a telephone that rings.

You may wonder, *But how do you find solitude with small children?* It's not easy, although with persistence you can, even though the solitude may seem brief. Perhaps you can take a few moments for a nap or quiet time when the children are in their beds. Late at night or in the early morning when everyone else is asleep may be a time that works for you. A Scripture verse written on a card, posted above the sink, can provide a spiritual vitamin. Or maybe you can take a prayer walk, stopping to study the sky and silently worship, lifting your cares and praise to God.

My mother told me that one night, when all seven of us children were small, she went outside and looked up into the star-filled night sky. She prayed in despair, "God, my life is so hectic, there's no way I can really study the Bible or pray as I should. How can I ever grow in you?" She told me that at that moment, she had a quiet assurance from

God that her heart's being turned to him was all that mattered. It was okay. She could do the best she could—it was her heart direction that mattered. He understands who we are and where we are in life.

Make Sure You Get Fed

However we do it, it's important to feed ourselves spiritually. By that I mean taking responsibility to have our own quiet time, to learn and grow.

When Joshua and his leaders finally crossed over the Jordan, he instructed them to "prepare provisions for yourselves, for within three days you will cross over this Jordan, to go in to possess the land which the LORD your God is giving you to possess" (Josh. 1:11).

In order to go on to possess the land—to achieve what God is calling us to—we must make sure to have provisions for ourselves, to feed ourselves. This is what helps us develop a life message with substance. Otherwise, even though we may be very busy, our lives will lack depth, no matter what our field or occupation. It is so important to be plugged into a church. The body of Christ is where we learn Scripture from teaching and from others. But beyond that, we need personal time to think about what we've heard and what we've read in the Bible. We need quiet places to honestly ask, How do I apply these Scriptures to my life? How does it change me?

In our First Callings—when life is all about making a living and caring for our growing families—it seems there is never enough time. If there is one piece of advice I would give young mothers, it is to get involved in a good Bible study—one that provides child care. If your schedule does not permit that, do the best you can to establish a time when you can read a devotional or some Scripture, and write your prayers and thoughts after you read. This helps you reflect on what you are reading. At a time when you are nourishing so many others, some kind of study of the Bible is an essential part of feeding yourself.

But we all want and need a purpose, a reason to live—something true, something solid. In our marketing and image-driven world, perception can take on a bigger life than the real deal. Al Ries and Jack Trout, in their book *Twenty-two Immutable Laws of Marketing,* say that one of those laws of marketing is perception.[6] The product may not be the best, but it must be perceived as the best. We are amused and entertained by much that isn't real. Reality TV shows play into our fantasies.

When it comes to having a purpose in our lives, perception isn't enough. Image isn't enough. Perception is like cotton candy: It evaporates before we even get to it. At our very core, we all long for something real to hold on to.

Pilate asked Jesus, "What is truth?" Jesus said, "I am the way, the truth and the life."

What Does Your Life Say?

> You are not only making memories . . . you are the memory!
>
> Phyllis Thoreau, *Night Lights*

It's freeing to understand that it's okay to be who you are. Your life is your major work. This is something I am only now appreciating. I used to think that to speak, to write books, I needed to generate knowledge from other places and use that material to speak to others. But I've learned that the only real material I have to deal with is my life and what God is doing in me.

It is the same with you and your one-of-a-kind life. When we spend time in God's Word and in prayer, and in honest journaling and in honest dialogue with others, giving out of the women God is making us is the most effective way to share the message of our lives. The question we must ask ourselves is, What is the message of my life that is contributing to make my corner of the world more beautiful?

My passionate quilting friends put pieces together to make a beautiful spread. And it's *for* something—it's warm and comforting and leaves a legacy.

That is what we want our life message to be—*for something*. As our lives unfold in the simplest, most common ways, God speaks to us through the stories of our lives—our successes and failures, tragedies and triumphs, in sicknesses and health, in interruptions and surprises.

What's Your Story?

> Child . . . I am telling you your story, not hers. I tell no one any story but his own.
>
> C. S. Lewis, *The Horse and His Boy*

While you have a story that is uniquely yours, it takes time and patience to develop it. Just as women gather around to help piece a quilt together, we gather around in circles of friendship and tell each other our stories. Learning and sharing with each other gives us strength, insight, and comfort. All stories have a beginning, as we all have beginnings. In the beginning, God created the earth. When I sit down to read to my four-year-old granddaughter, Kendsy, the story often begins: "Once upon a time. . . ." And so we begin, with high hopes and dreams.

Although my story begins with my birth, my story as a wife and mother began about thirty-six years ago, when I was eighteen and madly in love with a twenty-three-year-old graduate student. We began to date in January, and by February, he'd asked me to marry him. He was ready to move on in life, and I didn't want to lose him, so I said yes. *I can finish school later,* I thought. The future stretched out before me with unlimited possibilities. I didn't know much about life, but I was eager to learn.

My qualifications? I could play some classical music. I'd taken three years of French and could type one hundred words per minute. I had perfected the art of baking chocolate-chip cookies. That about filled my résumé. I was very taken with Bill's strong leadership abilities, his ambitions, and his dreams. I loved his sense of humor, his beautiful tenor voice, his devotion to his family.

So on August 20, 1966, Bill and I pledged our love to one another in my home church in Conrad, Montana. Thus began an adventure that would produce five amazing children: four sons and one daughter (plus three daughters-in-law and more to come!). Our adventure involved Bill's being a pastor of a church and shared work in publishing and writing and speaking. When my story as a married woman and mother began, I had no idea how consuming and defining it would be.

The First Calling—that time in life when we are young and are developing our passions, going to school, choosing a career, marrying, and having children—is a powerful, formative time. As I look back, it went quickly.

Beneath Your Message: His Love

This past Christmas was our first in our new house. We sold our family home after twenty-three years and built a new, smaller, empty-nest house just in time for our second son's wedding. *What a year,* I thought as I tried to plan for Christmas. Digging out the Christmas decorations, I came across some journals I'd kept sporadically when our four sons were under eight. I read through them, struck by the difference in my thinking then from now. My father was dying the Christmas I was thirty, which made it a bittersweet time. *Where did those years go*, I wondered. *Who was that young, idealistic woman?*

I sat in the loveseat, reading. I didn't have time for such aimless pursuits, yet I was fascinated as I looked across the span of years. I put the journals back in the box and stared out the windows as the snow filtered down, suddenly aware how different that long-ago Christmas was from this one. Yet, in some ways, it felt the same.

That snowy afternoon, big changes were taking place as we went through the traditions of shopping, addressing Christmas cards, baking. Christmas seemed almost bittersweet this year too. We were excited about having the family come home to the new house, but it had been hard to leave our family home crammed full of memories. *I have much to be thankful for!* I reminded myself. *So why this ache in my heart?*

I thought of Christmases when the children were small and found myself wishing we'd had more children, or that I'd waited longer to have them and that they'd still be home—all a postponement of the inevitable change and loss. *You can't stop time*, I thought. *You just have to get on it and ride, letting it take you to the next place.*

That holiday season, our children were in that fascinating stage of choosing life mates; our oldest and his wife were expecting their third child soon. There was the juggle of sharing holidays with extended family and in-laws. The circle widens as the children leave home, returning now and then through phone calls and holidays to touch base.

What could I say to young mothers, knowing what I do now? Savor every moment with your children. The frenetic cleaning, some of the social events you're so concerned about are not as important as just being there for your family. Just the time to play and laugh and have spontaneous fun is so good. If life gets too scheduled, you miss it.

Is it hard? You bet it is! It's not glamorous work. But what you're doing now has lifelong, eternal value. Be aware of those teachable moments. Time at Sunday school and vacation Bible school, praying with and reading to your children is important. Listen to them and realize that the conversations you have with them along the way help them develop spiritually too. You are concerned with their physical, emotional, and intellectual development, but as you are feeding them physically, you have a prime opportunity to feed them spiritually as well. What they will remember more than anything is you—not necessarily what you say.

That afternoon, as I was getting ready for Christmas and got sidetracked reading my old journals, I realized how quickly the years went, and I was overwhelmed with gratitude for my children. I had an irresistible urge to telephone each one (although I didn't!). Can you imagine their getting a phone call at work from their mother, saying, "I just wanted to tell you I love you, you wonderful person, you! Do you know how fabulous you are? Yeah, I know you're not perfect, but neither am I—and I just wanted to thank you for the privilege of being your mother."

Today our marriage is changing from a child-centered one to a couple-centered one, which is surprisingly wonderful. (And I have to admit that my role as Nana is my best gig right now!) The changes reminded me, on that snow-white day, that the message God writes upon our lives happens moment by moment, day by ordinary day. His love and faithfulness form the constant, defining thread that runs throughout our lives, through all seasons.

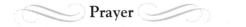 **Prayer**

Lord, sometimes in our day-to-day existence we are unaware that we are developing a story that gives a message. May our hearts be turned toward you. May we find a place somehow in the busyness and rush of

*life to hear your voice. May we learn what it means to
respect and honor you above all else and then to live a
life defined by that priority. In Christ's name, amen.*

Mapping Your Next Step

Read Proverbs 31, then prayerfully consider what qualities
you admire in that woman. Think on how can you help
develop those qualities in your own life.

- What do you think the message of your life is so far?
  What do you want it to be?
- Think of someone you admire—a role model or someone you would like to be like. What is the message
  of his or her life, and how do you think that message
  was shaped?
- Try to sum up your story in two paragraphs (who you
  are, where you were raised, if you are married, if you
  have children or work experience).
- What important choices have helped to shape the
  message that you are living today?
- How are changes affecting your life now?
- Share three goals that you have now (short-term and
  long-range goals).

3

What's My Work?

Mary and Martha:
The Important Work

If you can't be a highway, then just be a trail,
If you can't be the sun, be a star;
It isn't by size that you win or you fail—
Be the best of whatever you are!

Douglas Malloch (1705–1765)

Being a hostess was Martha's thing—she was famous for it in Bethany and even beyond. People said if you wanted a fantastic meal, Martha was the one to fix it. An invitation to her home for dinner was an experience you didn't miss. With her creative touch and imagination, she could make the most ordinary food memorable. But it wasn't just the meal—it was the setting. She knew what it took: fresh flowers placed just so, the right wine, comfortable conversation, the room spotless yet inviting. She knew how to keep hot food hot and cold food cold and always added some surprising twist to the meal that was delicious, unexpected.

When it was time to serve, she knew how to coordinate everything to be ready at the same time. The morning of her dinner, she went to the marketplace to be sure she got the freshest vegetables, fruits, and herbs for seasoning. Yes, it took work, but she wasn't afraid of work. Work was how good things happened.

Her sister, Mary, lived with her. Mary was sweet, but she could be a bit absentminded at times. She was quiet, a thinker. Then there was that day when their dearest friend, Jesus, came to visit. He'd been there before, but this time Martha told him that he should consider their home his. After all, he didn't really have a home—he lived like a vagabond, ministering to crowds of people, healing them, teaching them. Martha knew how exhausted he must be, not having a place to call his own. Everybody needed something from Jesus—well, she'd be different! She would take care of him and see that he got a delicious, nourishing meal and a good night's rest.

That day, she knocked herself out more than usual. She got up early and cleaned the house from top to bottom, scrubbing everything so that all was in order. She hurried to the market to buy the food and then home to bake fresh bread and begin roasting the meat.

Finally Jesus came. Mary brought him in and washed his feet while Martha brought him a cool drink. How they loved him, and how honored and excited they were to have him as their friend.

Martha went back to the kitchen to finish the meal while Mary visited with Jesus. The menu she'd planned was elaborate; in fact, she'd never made that dish before, but this was for Jesus. The sauce for the meat wasn't turning out quite the way it was supposed to, and Martha began to get flustered. Perspiration stuck to her robe. On her fifth trip to the table to put the condiments in place, she glanced over at Mary. What was wrong with her? Couldn't Mary see she needed help? Usually she was ready to serve, but when Martha needed her most, she was totally oblivious. Martha tried to catch her eye, but there she sat, listening intently to what Jesus was saying, now and then asking a thoughtful question.

Martha stormed back to the kitchen, hoping Mary would take the hint, but it was as if she didn't even exist. Oh, she'd wanted this to be such a wonderful meal for Jesus, to let him know how special he was! As she went back to the table with the fresh bread, Jesus looked up. Martha couldn't help herself and exclaimed plaintively, "Lord, don't you care that my sister has left me to do the work by myself? Tell her to help me!" (Luke 10:40 NIV).

Then Jesus spoke to her with that knowing love, a tender smile on his face. "Martha, Martha, you are worried and troubled about many things. But one thing is needed, and Mary has chosen that good part, which will not be taken away from her" (Luke 10:41–42).

Well, okay! Finally the meal was ready, and they sat together, eating. The wonderful food she'd tried so hard to fix didn't seem so wonderful. Exhausted, she leaned back and tried to listen.

What We Can Learn from Mary and Martha

Remember Your Most Important Priority

It seems to me that Martha's theme could be "If it's going to be, it's up to me!" Or "If it's going to be done right, I'd better do it." Later, when Mary and Martha's brother, Lazarus, got sick, they sent for Jesus, but Lazarus died before Jesus got there. At the aforementioned dinner, the complaint from her overworked self was "Don't you care that I'm doing this all alone?" When Lazarus died, she accused, "If you'd been here, Lazarus wouldn't have died!" In other words, "Jesus, do you really care about me? Or am I out here on my own, trying to make things happen?"

From Martha's words we can assume that she felt alone, let down—perhaps victimized at times. It was up to her to make good things happen. I can relate to Martha, and I know these are bad feelings to have. There have been times when I knocked myself out for acceptance and approval, and then when people didn't come through for me, I was left feeling angry and resentful—a sure recipe for stress. Stress is not "out there"; it's "in here."

Don't misunderstand me: Hard work is good, and to get important things done, sometimes we have seasons of plain stubborn effort. I'm sure Jesus ate and enjoyed that meal. But motives are important. What drives us? Those of us with a strong streak of perfectionism would rather do it ourselves than risk it being imperfect. Jesus saw Martha's anxieties and reminded her of her most important priority.

Make Jesus at Home in Your Life

At Lazarus's grave, Jesus told Martha, "Your brother will rise again." Martha replied, "I know that he will rise again in the resurrection at the last day." Then Jesus said those spectacular words to Martha that have comforted so many of his followers through the ages: "I am the resurrection and the life. He who believes in Me, though he may die, he shall live. And whoever lives and believes in Me shall never die. Do you believe this?" Martha replied with a statement of faith that preceded the amazing miracle of Jesus' raising Lazarus from the dead: "Yes, Lord, I believe that You are the Christ, the Son of God, who is to come into the world" (John 11:23–27).

It seemed that Martha had turned the corner. What it comes down to is believing him, trusting him to do the real work. We do what we can, and sometimes it's a lot.

But the point is to hear Jesus' words, do what he says, and trust him with results. Jesus affirmed Mary for her choice to listen, but he also loved Martha. He saw her heart—her anxiety about many things and the drive for perfection, for acceptance through good works.

I too want Jesus to be at home in my life, just as Martha wanted him to have a good meal, to feel at home. Martha loved Jesus. She believed in him, and she wanted to serve him. But sometimes, like Martha, I get all caught up in the work and forget about listening to Jesus. Our work can be a consuming thing. And like Martha, I'm not afraid of work. I know what it takes: clean, vacuum, dust. Decorate, redecorate. Shop, cook, clean it up, then start all over again. Or organize an event: sell tickets, serve on committees, plan the food, the speakers, and so on and so on.

Women's work is unique and important. Say what you will about contemporary roles of men and women, there's something about the woman's touch that is quite magical. We women are good at details, at knowing what has to happen in order for families to get nourished, holidays and traditions to become established, events made memorable, houses furnished and decorated, relationships cared for and celebrated. Or, to put it bluntly, to get income earned.

I remember standing with my mother in the funeral home as she said good-bye to my grandmother. She touched her mother's hands and said, "She worked so hard." Indeed, she did. Widowed young with four children in the Depression years, she worked at all kinds of jobs: cleaning houses for people, baby-sitting, cooking for farm crews to make money. She had no choice but to find whatever work she could, and many women are in that situation today. The reality is that for most of us, work's not a hobby; it's a necessity. I remember my grandmother saying, "You can't be so heavenly minded you're no earthly good!" But in her later years, my grandmother became a voracious reader of the Bible. She lived most of her life as a Martha, but toward the end of her life, she studied and learned from Jesus as Mary did.

Don't Miss Your Real Calling

In America, we live in a culture that values *doing* and not *being*. We are more concerned with quantity rather than quality, with the stimulation of constant activity rather than substance. We often judge ourselves and others on what we have accomplished, rather than on who we are. It's easy to become addicted to achievement because of the powerful payoff: acceptance and approval. How important it is to honor those quiet places in the midst of life to make sure our work is our calling.[1]

I sit here, staring at my stacks of books and notes. This book writing business is hard work; it can be intense and consuming. Today my work is writing about the importance of relationships, how this is our true work. While I'm trying to finish the book, I am neglecting some relationships. Oh yes, Martha and I have a lot in common. She's frantic about serving Jesus, and I am frantic about getting this book written. And Mary—who seems to be doing nothing—gets Jesus' recognition! We work for different reasons. There is the undeniable and necessary matter of making a living. And it's also true that our work can be a joyful living out of our calling.

At certain moments, when I'm stuck on a chapter or get that writer's block, I think, *What am I doing, writing all this lofty stuff? I need to be living it. That's where the important work is.* But then I get a phone call or a note from someone who tells me what I wrote and said made a difference, which helps me understand that writing is part of the work of my life. But it's possible to be so focused on the work of writing that I miss my real calling—which is to sit at Jesus' feet and then live and write out of that reality. As my friend

Nita told me, "I have simplified my goals to focus not on the calling but on the *Caller*."

What's in Store for You and Me?

> I believe that what woman resents is not so much giving herself in pieces as giving herself purposelessly.
>
> Anne Morrow Lindbergh, *Gift from the Sea*

Donald Clifton and Paula Nelson, in their book, *Soar with Your Strengths*, describe some practical ways that we can understand what our work is. They say to "find out what you do well and do more of it!"[2] Look at your natural abilities and things you do that come easily for you. Everyone has that thing he or she does best—the thing that can make you lose track of time when you're engaged in it. It's where you really come alive.

Rick Warren, in his excellent book *The Purpose Driven Life*, says that your heart is your passion—that which you love reveals the true you. He writes:

> What I am able to do, God wants me to do. . . . To discover God's will for your life, you should seriously examine what you are good at doing and what you're not good at. If God hasn't given you the ability to carry a tune, he isn't going to expect you to be an opera singer. God will never ask you to dedicate your life to a task you have no talent for. On the other hand, the abilities you do have are a strong indicator of what God wants you to do with your life.[3]

Listen for Yearnings

Something deep inside you says, *I'd love to do that! I could do that!* It's something that keeps coming up in your thinking. Look back to when you were very young. What were the hobbies, the things you loved to do? Most likely, they were a reflection of your giftedness.

Watch for Satisfaction

This is where emotional and psychological rewards are great. One day Bill and I were teaching some college-aged young people a class on relationships at George Fox University. As I was talking to them, the look on their faces struck me—they were listening. I had an incredible sense that this was the most satisfying work anyone could ever ask for: to teach young people hungry to know.

Watch for Rapid Learning

If you catch on to something easily, you're likely to be good at it. My husband is skillful at developing property and houses. When he was very young, he worked with his father, who was a building contractor. Bill learned quickly to draw plans to scale and then to see the whole project completed from those plans. What kind of projects or work energizes you? That is most likely an indication of your strength. What kind of project or work drains you, bores you? That would most likely indicate something you should avoid.

Your Focus: Relationships

Women's work seems more fragmented than men's. We have to be so many different things to so many different people. It's pretty hard to define our work, we who care for our families. For one thing, it seems we women never stop cleaning, no matter what else we do in life. I just talked to my eighty-one-year-old mother-in-law, who was cleaning closets. Bill's mother's work now is caring for herself and her ninety-one-year-old husband (although he will tell you his work is caring for her!). As long as we live, it seems we are cleaning up our own and others' messes. Someone once said that for a woman, a vacation means a different sink! I look around my house this morning and realize it definitely needs attention. But what is my real work?

From the response I've received from women I've surveyed, it seems very clear that regardless of our occupations, our work centers around relationships. While men seem to define their lives by their careers—and many of us women love our jobs too—we most clearly define ourselves through our constantly changing, fluid relationships.

Some years ago, when we had four little boys under eight, Bill took a job with a missions organization and was away from home a great deal. In my previous life as a pastor's wife, I had taught a Bible study and was very involved in people's lives. More to the point, I had an identity as the pastor's wife. For Bill's new job, we'd had to move to a new city, a new house, a new neighborhood.

One afternoon shortly after we'd moved, I was standing in front of the kitchen sink, wondering, *What on earth am I doing here? I feel so isolated. Bored.* I missed all the people who had been important to us. I questioned, *Whatever happened to my dreams, my passions? I was going to become a writer and travel widely. Now I'm doing good to write a grocery list and get to the store.* I prayed, "Lord, I need a ministry that will make a difference in somebody's life. I need something to really sink my teeth into!"

At that very moment, my son Christian, who was three at the time, tugged on my jeans. He had a game in his hand and asked, "Mommy, will you play this with me?" It was quite clear that God was saying, "So you want something that will make a difference in somebody's life? A ministry to really sink your teeth into? Well, look behind you!" I began to fall in love with my children in a new way, to embrace my work as a mother. Looking back, I know those were wonderful, fulfilling years.

Yes, I had other interests. I taught a women's Bible study in our new church and made new friends. I supported my husband in his calling. But mainly, for almost two decades, my children filled my world, and I began writing out of that life. Being a mother is an all-enveloping, holy, and difficult calling. Perhaps you've been there, in the trenches. Or you are there now. Once in a while you get a glimpse of the rewards, which you celebrate and treasure because they're rare. I had such a reward the other day.

As I was cleaning my desk, I found two pages of a handwritten letter on plain notepaper tucked inside a folder. I recognized it as a letter Chris wrote me a few years ago for the first Mother's Day he was away from home at college. He wrote,

> Mom. One of the earliest memories I have is one of you trying to teach me our phone number. Although the phone number itself I have forgotten, I do remember you encouraging me. You said, "That's right! Good!" I remember feeling proud of myself. Many mothers try to teach their children phone numbers for simple safety precautions, as I'm sure you were also doing. But not many do so with love like you do (and did). You were building self-esteem within me. Thank you, Mom. . . . I guess the only way to ever repay you is to one day give to my children what you and Dad have given me . . . and that is Jesus . . . and love . . . and faith . . . and kindness.

It moved me deeply to know that my son saw Jesus in me, in spite of my weaknesses and failures. How we need those moments of encouragement.

Watch the Work Deepen

An unknown writer said, "One of the most insidious temptations that confronts any Christian is to gain applause. It is so easy to temper our actions so as to have the approval of the crowd." Work is a wonderful, God-given gift, but it can have a negative side. I know mine: the tendency to work for love. Like Martha, I can work like crazy to make Jesus feel at home and end up having no time for him. I can work like crazy for my children, only to have them leave! Since my work is centered around relationships, and relationships change, what is my work when the work changes? It does change, little by little. We stop nursing. Our children grow up and come home occasionally for holidays and special gatherings. Then we pull out all the stops to get ready for the family. In other words, *Shop! Bake! Slice and dice!* Then they leave again.

Recently I thought of the painful day, not too many years ago, when my sisters and I helped our mother, who was suffering from Alzheimer's, pack her belongings so she could move to a care facility. Somehow, boxing up her kitchen was almost more difficult than her funeral nine months later, because it seemed to define so clearly who she was to us: nurturer. Preparing and serving food is symbolic of giving, of nurturing, of caring—a powerful symbol of life—nourishment we need to go on. It is something we wives and mothers do that makes us indispensable.

It seemed unthinkable for Mother not to have a kitchen. We packed the familiar utensils and dishes that had accumulated over the years: her worn-out mixer, the cookbooks with the splotches on the best recipes, her big wooden bowl that we'd served salad in hundreds of times, the teacups she'd collected through the years, her Wedgwood china. Her kitchen represented so much of her work of caring for her family, and that part of her life was over.

Now that she's been gone for almost ten years, I see the whole scope of her life, and it certainly was bigger than her kitchen. What stays with me? Her smile, her laughter. Her spontaneous poetry quotes. Her love of finding new truths in God's Word and explaining them to anyone who would listen. Her wonder at beauty: the sky, flowers, and birds. Her delight in each of her children and grandchildren.

All the work she did was incidental. What lasts is her wonderful, imperfect personality and knowing that she loved us. My sister Janie describes her this way: "Mom led us; taught us; and those treasures are still in our hearts, bearing fruit. A thing of beauty never escaped her notice, from a baby's smile to a clump of wildflowers in a field. Life was a series of wonderful adventures—always something new to learn, to see, and to experience. In her priorities of interest, God was first; her family, second; and the whole world, third."

For Us All: Mary and Martha 101

First, we must not compare our approach to life to another's. Jesus sees our hearts, and people do life differently. My sister Kitty is an incredible woman. She is a great cook and caters many weddings and events. More than that, she loves Jesus and people and serves out of loving them, often taking meals to people who are sick. I could never do what she does, but it is her calling, and she does it well and with joy.

Second, we can't let things become more important than people. Deborah's daughter was marrying a young man from an upscale family, and two days before the wedding, Deborah and her husband hosted the groom's family for a dinner. Deborah told me she was a nervous wreck: "All I could think about was how inadequate my home and meal must look compared to theirs. I'm usually a good cook, and I made my specialty for dessert, apple pie. Wouldn't you know, it burned on the bottom! I couldn't believe it. It was a terrible night. I couldn't enjoy getting to know these people at all because I was so tied in knots. Later they sent a kind note, [saying] how much they enjoyed being with us, and so on. Now that I look back, I wish I had just fixed something simpler and focused on getting to know them."

Third, Martha's work is valuable, but what carries us through all seasons is a Mary heart. We should be both Mary and Martha in our lives. Work is good. We need it. But there's a deeper component to our work, a thoughtful aspect. Mary represents the importance of solitude in our lives. We work, but we must do so out of that quiet place before God. That's what gives our work meaning.

My friend Linda Swearingen is an incredibly gifted, visionary woman. She married a high school teacher while very young and had two children. Filled with boundless energy and enthusiasm, she first became a realtor in her small town, then got involved in the city council; from there she became mayor. While her children were still at home, she finished her master's degree and maintained an interest in policy and government. One thing led to another, and she ran for county commissioner.

She was popular and headed for big-time success in government. She had the right connections to be a difference maker, as well as the unique ability to enjoy and appreciate people as well as get things done. I valued her ability to achieve personal goals and asked her to go with me on a weekend women's prison outreach to teach a session out of her experiences. She will tell you that God broke her heart that weekend for women in crisis and reshaped her life—and showed her where her true work was. She had a Mary experience and heard from Jesus.

Now, two years later, she has started a nonprofit ministry, Bridge to Hope, that helps women transition from prison to a productive life. It is a truly effective ministry that is only one of a handful being considered as faith-based initiatives on a national level.

Each woman has a work, a purpose that produces something, and it's not just mindless activity. Women's work is wonderful! Exult in it. Savor it! Take great satisfaction in it. But what makes it truly significant is when Jesus is at home in our work and we listen to him.

Each one of us is unique, and God has a calling for us. We know instinctively that we are created for something. Outside on my deck, a mother bird and father bird have built a nest and are now busy carrying insects to feed their hungry brood. No one had to tell them what their purpose was, and I doubt they sat on a tree branch and agonized and analyzed what could be their calling. Their Creator built their purpose into them, and they simply live it.

We can relax in him, knowing that he leads us to create, to work, to honor him in our changing lives. Our chief work is to love him, and out of that relationship, live joyfully, knowing that we are his workmanship—and that he won't forsake the work of his hands.

Prayer

Lord, sometimes my life feels chaotic, as I must be many things to many different people. But sometimes my busyness is, I confess, a way to avoid listening to you and to my own life. It's easier to fuss around and blame others. But here I am, now, sitting at your feet—and I am listening. My life is in your hands. I want to do your will. You know what's best, and I long to do the work you have for me, work that blesses and helps others. Amen.

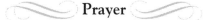

Mapping Your Next Step

Read the story of Mary and Martha in Luke 10.

- Which woman do you most identify with, and why?
- Why do you think Martha was feeling anxious?

- Why is perfectionism not a good thing? What about it is good?

Ask yourself these questions for clues to your calling:

- What activity or project really makes me come alive?
- What hobbies or things that I collect give me a clue as to my calling?
- What projects or events energize me? (Do more of this!)
- What projects or events drain me? (Do less of this!)
- What steps can I take to be more fully engaged with my calling?
- How can Jesus be at home in my work?

4

Taking Inventory

The Widow in 2 Kings 4:
Discovering Her One True Thing

The great Master said, "I see no best in kind, but in
  degree;
I gave a various gift to each, to charm, to strengthen,
  and to teach."

Henry Wadsworth Longfellow, *The Singers*

Things had started out great for them. Her husband had
a keen interest in the things of God and enrolled in
the school of the prophets under Elisha. Although it cost
them dearly, they both felt it was worth the extra expense.
Surely God will provide if we seek him first, they reasoned.
They had two young sons, and life was good—that is, until
her husband became very ill one evening. She tried to nurse
him to health, but he was burning up with fever and had
an agonizing pain in his side. She prayed continually for
God to heal him as she bathed him with cool water.

Her neighbor made a special brew of bitter herbs, hoping it would help, but her husband only got worse. In just a few days, the unthinkable happened—he died. She was devastated. How could such a thing be? How could she raise their two sons alone? And why did God let this happen when they were trying to learn more about him and his ways?

A few days after his burial, as she sorted out their business affairs, she discovered to her dismay that they owed a large amount of money. Their creditor came by one afternoon. He looked at her sons carefully. Both of them were just entering their teens, and she did not like the way he looked at them. He told her in a quiet voice that if she sold her sons to him as slaves, he would consider all her debts satisfied.

That did it. Eyes blazing, she insisted he leave—immediately. Then she went to Elisha. After all, he was the one who had so impressed her husband. She told him: "Your servant my husband is dead, and you know that he revered the LORD. But now his creditor is coming to take my two boys as his slaves!" Elisha asked, "How can I help you? Tell me, what do you have in your house?" (2 Kings 4:1–2 NIV).

"Your servant has nothing there at all," she said, "except a little oil" (2 Kings 4:3 NIV). That's when Elisha told her to do something quite ridiculous—but she was desperate and willing to try anything. What did she have to lose? He told her to send her sons to all the neighbors and borrow empty vessels—"Not a few," he said. He told her to bring them into her house with her two sons, shut the door, and begin pouring oil from her small jar into the empty ones. And she did exactly that.

An amazing thing happened: The oil just kept coming. Her sons were so excited; they were jumping up and down and laughing as they kept bringing her the empty jars to fill. She exclaimed, "Bring me another vessel!" And her son said, "Mom, that's it—there aren't any more." And the oil stopped flowing. She was able to sell all the oil for a good sum, enough to satisfy their debt.

What an incredible experience, and what an up close and personal miracle for her sons to witness. After all, their freedom was at stake, so they had a vested interest in this miracle!

What We Can Learn from the Widow in 2 Kings

Inventory by Starting Where You Are

The question we all must answer when it comes to taking an inventory of our lives is the one Elisha asked the young widow: What do you have in your house? God always starts with where we are and what we have. I find this woman's response interesting. What did she have in her house? Of course, she had all kinds of things—she had been married some years and had a family. Yet her first response is like many of ours: "Your servant has nothing there at all . . . except a little oil." Perhaps she was thinking of what could be marketable, of use to the world, something that would give her a little power and leverage. Life can throw us some unexpected turns. Just at a time in life when we most need to be productive, we feel bankrupt, useless.

We look around at others who seem to have so much more than we do—more talent, more ability, more resources—and it seems that we really don't have anything. And yet the probing question comes to each of us: What do you have?

Reconsider All Your Material Possessions

Stuff, I call it. When we went through our move last year, I was shocked at all the stuff. One night, even though it was still dark, I was suddenly wide awake. Trying not to disturb my husband's sleep, I put on my robe and slippers and went out to a loveseat near the bay window, where I usually have my coffee and quiet time.

The woodstove still had embers glowing, and I sat down with my reading and notebook. I realized why I was awake. We were moving in three days. How on earth was I going to get everything done? I had been packing for weeks, sorting, throwing out, and giving things away. It was shocking to realize how much stuff we had crammed into one house after twenty-three years and five children. In the back of my closet, I found a box of my wedding announcements (thirty-five years old)! There were countless items from my children: notebooks, photos, lettermen's jackets, trophies, baseball cards.

As I sat and began to read, I heard a strange, intermittent wheezing sound. I looked around and saw nothing. What could it be? I went back to my reading, and again I heard it, like something was being dragged across the floor. I finally got up and began to search, feeling almost frightened in the semidarkened house. And then I saw it—a frog, of all things, in the dining room, all tangled up with some old, dried poinsettia leaves. It took me a few moments to recognize what it was. What a strange sight! The leaves covered him as he worked hard to cross the floor. He must have gotten in through an open door as we'd been moving things in and out, and he apparently got wrapped up in poinsettia leaves that had fallen behind some furniture after Christmas.

Since I've been known to beg my husband to kill spiders for me, I thought about waking Bill. But he'd been working so hard, I didn't have the heart to wake him. I reminded myself that I was a grown woman, so I grabbed the dustpan, and after some maneuvering, I coaxed the frog onto it and threw him outside on the deck. He shook off the old leaves and hopped vigorously away. Poor little thing, dragging those leaves around.

I realized with a smile that maybe that's what God was doing for me—trying to set me free from dragging all the stuff around. Sometimes the more cluttered our lives are, the emptier they seem. I thought of my blithe statement to people who asked why we were selling our house: "The house is to facilitate the life; we are not here to maintain the house. We feel God is calling us to simplify our lives." *Yeah, right,* I thought with some irony. The whole process is certainly not simple. It's much easier to keep hanging on to everything, adding and adding and adding. But it's not efficient, and it's not being a good steward of what God's given to us. So there I was, trying to inventory: What do I have? What do I keep? What do I need for the future?

We all have material possessions. But the more stuff we have, the more care and attention and time it takes to manage it, clean it, store it, and use it. It's possible to spend our lives being defined by and managing stuff. The rich young ruler who went to Jesus asked what he needed to do to have eternal life, and Jesus told him to sell all that he had and follow him. The rich young ruler turned away sorrowful—because he had too much (Luke 18:18–23). It hindered him.

We may be in a wonderful place when we answer, "I have nothing . . . except . . ." Dr. Paul Tournier, a renowned Swiss psychiatrist whose writings are out of print but nonetheless profound, wrote how suffering and deprivation are the most fertile places for creativity to take place.[1] In our needs and in our emptiness, life is stripped down to its cleanest component, and we can see amidst the clutter what is worth keeping. The young widow found it: her oil.

Talents: Put Them to Use

For the kingdom of heaven is like a man traveling to a far country, who called his own servants and delivered his goods to them. And to one he gave five talents, to another

two, and to another one, to each according to his own
ability. . . . For to everyone who has, more will be given,
and he will have abundance; but from him who does not
have, even what he has will be taken away.

Matthew 25:14–15, 29

What is your oil? What talent do you possess, even though
you may see it as insignificant or "nothing"? You know
what it is, even though you may have to think a bit. Perhaps you have the talent of encouragement, and you could
spend some time on Saturdays making someone's day with
a friendly visit. It may be that you have some musical ability.
Or you enjoy teaching, and nothing makes you feel more
fulfilled than to see the lights go on in your student's eyes
as he or she "gets it." You may have a talent for understanding finances, and you get great satisfaction out of setting
up a workable budget. It may be your outgoing personality,
and you are good with people. My friend Connie says that
being a "friend maker" is her talent. Though she has many
gifts, that is truly where she shines. Her talent is an asset
to her husband, who heads a national company that helps
finance churches.

But what you have is not the point—it's whether you
will see your gifts and talents and then willingly offer them
to him. It really is true: Little is much in God's hands. The
young boy gave his lunch of five barley loves and two fish
to Jesus, and as Jesus blessed and broke it, his small lunch
fed thousands (see John 6:1–3).

When we give what we have to him, as insignificant as
we think it is, he multiplies it. It's interesting to see that
although Elisha knew what the widow needed—money
to get out of debt—he asked her a question, forced her to
articulate her need. "What do you want me to do for you?"
he asked. And then he asked what she had in her house.

God has made each of us with certain gifts and talents,
and it's important to realize that they lie within us—they

71

are not something we have to generate from outside. Niccolo Paganini (1782–1840), one of the greatest violinists of all time, was about to perform before a sold-out opera house. He walked on the stage to a huge ovation and felt that something was terribly wrong. Suddenly he realized that he had someone else's violin in his hands. Horrified, but knowing that he had no other choice, he began to play. That day he gave the performance of his life. Afterward Paganini reflected to a fellow musician, "Today, I learned the most important lesson of my career. Before today, I thought the music was in the violin; today I learned that the music is in me."[2]

Use Those Connections

We all have connections. The young widow used what she had—her oil—and then used her connections—her neighbors. She had evidently developed good relationships with them and went to them to borrow the empty vessels. Some people may already have "vessels"—the resources, education, or financial backing. She did not have any of those, but she had something just as valuable: She had her good name, her integrity, and her healthy relationships. She recognized these, and when she needed them most, used them.

Maybe the next step in your life is to further your education or to start a business, and you feel powerless to get there. Take a good look at your connections, some key relationships you have. Perhaps it's time for you to get some honest counsel from someone you respect. Or maybe it's time for you to take out a loan to launch your business or to finish your education. There are government, civic, and community service connections as well, not to mention church connections. These can be valuable assets.

I've come to realize I am a "connector." How do I know that? Because so many people call me for others' phone numbers, e-mail addresses, speaker recommendations, and so on. The other day, after the tenth such phone call, I started to feel annoyed. *What am I, a walking resource book?* Then the light went on—of course. I do know a lot of people, and I get a kick out of introducing them to each other. I enjoy my connections and making them for other people.

Evaluate Your Experiences

We all have experiences. Oh, do we ever. Experience is worth a lot, even if you feel you've failed at certain things. Perhaps it's a divorce or mistakes you think you made in raising your children. Along with all the important things we've learned, the failures and regrets are just as valuable to others—maybe more. We may wonder, *What do I have to offer? I've just been a wife and mother for twenty-five years. Or I've helped my family run a business. I've been doing the same thing for so long. Or I've been in full-time ministry for ten years, and I'm ready for something new.*

You most likely know more than you think you do. I always felt somewhat intimidated and at a disadvantage in various settings because instead of finishing college, I married young and began having babies early in my marriage. I was surprised one day when I got a letter from the president of Western Baptist College, inviting me, along with my husband, to receive an honorary doctorate because of my contribution to Christian writing. Later, I was invited to be on the board of trustees for George Fox University. I am also on the board of the ministry I mentioned in the last chapter that helps women transition from prison to productive life. I get great satisfaction from contributing to these causes because of my passion to connect Christ with the real world. But all that I contribute simply comes from my experience, from offering my perspective on situations—and offering what I have, such as it is. Po Branson writes, "Your experiences are your chance to define your meaning."[3]

I'm convinced that if you want to grow, you will become rich in experience. Life will just give it to you. My friend Ruth Lovegren filled her life with raising four children and helping her husband run a resort for more than thirty years. Unexpectedly, her husband died shortly after they sold their resort, and her hopes and dreams for retirement underwent radical reshaping. But now I see how productive Ruth's life is. Besides being a wonderful influence on her large extended family, she is involved in the local school and is an influential board member of a youth camp. From her years at the resort, she learned a great deal about working with the public, and her insights are invaluable. Not only that, she is a godly woman of prayer who has learned much about God and people through the years. She has come with me on speaking assignments, and her counsel and wisdom are invaluable to me personally, much of them generated out of her experiences.

Dream

Dream lofty dreams, and as you dream, so shall you become. The greatest achievement was at first and for a time a dream. The oak sleeps in the acorn; the bird waits in the egg; and in the highest vision of the soul a waking angel stirs. Dreams are the seedlings of realities.

James Allen

"Where there is no vision, the people perish" (Prov. 29:18 KJV). I believe that the young widow who needed a miracle had dreams. Her husband's death crushed those longings, and even more dreadful was the thought of losing her sons. But she had the initiative and persistence not to dwell in despair, and she went to Elisha for help. God's miraculous provision restored her life.

It's also worth noting that when she had filled the last empty vessel, the oil stopped flowing. She had faith for a certain amount of oil—her dreams went so far, and that was it. We often put limits on God, and we can let people pour cold water on our dreams. If you look at the life of an extraordinary person, you will see that she succeeded because she kept dreaming, kept believing for new possibilities, and kept offering an empty vessel to be filled.

One woman told me, "I don't really have any dreams." I think we all start out life with dreams—they are just built into us. Ask any child, "What do you want to be when you grow up?" and watch his eyes light up at the possibilities. Sometimes we neglect those dreams, or life derails them. I urge you to take an inventory of what you have, then offer it to God to restore, reshape, and redeem. Dreams, in this sense, are a form of optimism, food for our faith.

Some dreams are easier to realize than others. Some are more lofty, less accessible. Some dreams take longer than others. When I was twelve, I vividly remember huddling one night before the furnace in my long flannel nightgown, thinking: *Wouldn't it be great if someday I meet the man of my dreams? And we marry and have four or five children? And work for God somewhere . . . somehow help people?* Years later, I look back with gratitude. God gifted me with a caring husband, four sons, one daughter, and opportunities to help people. Living the dream hasn't always been easy, and it sometimes very narrowly defined my life. Yet I'm grateful for it and for the power of dreams.

A single woman, Naomi, who has been involved in teaching for years, told me, "I put my life on hold emotionally for so long, waiting for 'Mr. Wonderful,' who, by the way, never showed up. Then I realized God had another dream for me. I've stayed anchored in him and kept a sense of adventure. Now I am privileged to teach and mentor young people, and God and I are making a difference."

Ever since I was small, I had a very specific dream. *Someday*, said the longing deep inside of me, *I'll be a writer.* I kept diaries and journals all through school, into college and marriage. Then I quit. The early marriage years were hectic, and I shelved my dream for a while. Until one night.

We had just moved with our two small sons. The babies were both asleep, and Bill was at a meeting as I was sorting through boxes, putting things away. That's when I came across my journals in the bottom of a box—an odd assortment of notebooks and diaries that I'd kept since I was about twelve years old.

I remember hugging them like long-lost children, crying, "Where have you been? I've missed you so!" It was like finding my self again. I had sometimes felt that my soul had oozed through my fingertips into the diaper pail or dishwater. But there was concrete evidence that I had a self, that once I'd dreamed of being a writer.

I began journaling again, feeding the dream. There were many times, when my children were small, that my dreams were frustrated, delayed, or reshaped. I wondered at times, after I got a rejection letter, *Will I ever be a writer?* Yet as I persisted, I realized my dream.

My dream to go back to school to finish my education is one I have not realized. One day, when my children were all in school, I went to the local community college and signed up for the courses that would take me toward finishing my degree. I came home, looked at the calendar with our children's school and sports events and Bill's schedule, and decided there was no way I could do it. I called and canceled my enrollment. That was a choice I deliberately made, yet somehow, in the back of my mind, the possibility stays. Now people my age who are teaching are retiring, and I wonder if it's too late for me. Time will tell!

Maybe you wonder as I do: *How do I know this is a dream I should pursue? Is my dream God's dream? Or is it reshaped and given back in another way?*

Dreams come in many sizes. Dreams can be the small, hopeful inspirations that keep us growing and developing. I remember watching a close friend in her home, how easily she used her gifts of hospitality and homemaking. *I would love to do that too,* I thought. And watching her, I was able to grow in that area.

Dreams are important, but to realize a dream means putting legs to it. The young widow had to send her sons to borrow the empty vessels, and then she had to pour out of her own jar of oil. She didn't just sit there and think, *Well, I could have succeeded . . . maybe. But maybe not. If only money would just drop from the sky!* She risked looking silly and borrowed empty jars from her neighbors.

> Cherish your visions; cherish your ideals; cherish the music that stirs in your heart, the beauty that forms in your mind, the loveliness that drapes your purest thoughts; for out of them will grow all delightful conditions. "Ask and you shall receive."
>
> James Allen[4]

Let Your Life Inventory Begin!

How revealing it is to take an honest inventory of one's life. This hit home when I asked several groups of women to use the chart at the end of this chapter (see My Personal Inventory). The very exercise had an unexpected effect on some women.

While some women found great satisfaction in doing personal inventories of their lives and said it made them grateful, others began to cry—deep sobs. One woman could not even articulate her feelings. The emotions seemed to be centered around regrets, past mistakes. *All the time doing such worthless things to please some nameless, faceless entity. What was that for, anyway?*

The measuring stick for both groups of women were these things, which they agreed were very important:

Creativity—Expressing our selves through art, music, style, and communication ranked as very important.

Education—This also was at the top of the list for those women who were glad they'd done it; it also topped the list of regrets for those who hadn't finished.

Loved ones—Husbands, children, and extended family, as well as close friends, were all high priorities.

Personal fitness—Caring for our physical selves, especially if we are approaching midlife, has become an essential.

Spiritual relationship—The biggest challenge is living out of the primary connection with Jesus, the relationship we need to help us through our other relationships.

Know What to Delete

When you do an inventory, you inevitably see things you need to get rid of. Maybe it once served a purpose, but now it needs to go because it's cluttering your purpose. In order to live an efficient life, we must delete some things.

When we moved last year, I made so many trips to the local thrift shop, I developed friendships with the staff! Too much stuff can create confusion. When we take inventories of our lives and clear out some things, we can see what's valuable and what needs to go.

We all have time wasters that fill our days. A big one many women named is TV. Sometimes watching TV becomes a pacifier, they said. We plant ourselves on the couch or in a chair, and before we know it, we've spent several hours on a pastime that we can't even remember the next day.

There's no need to become legalistic about TV, and

certainly there are times when it's okay to "waste time," not to be so frenetic with the schedule. It's okay to take in maybe an hour of a good television show (or not feel guilty for sitting down to read a good book).

I'm talking about mindless, aimless things that have no real lasting value, things such as hours spent shopping or baking cookies when there's no one there to eat them but us, and we sure don't need them.

Sometimes we delete things that we wish later we'd kept. Knowing what to delete helps us know what to save.

One woman told me she had been doing work on her computer when she received the inventory I sent her. On her computer, she'd had to delete a lot of old messages, unnecessary spam that was coming into her e-mail. The question *Is there anything in your life you need to delete?* held fresh meaning for her. She realized she had deleted some relationships—not erased them, really—they'd been in her "save" file. In essence, she'd deleted them to "save." She made phone calls and took steps to restore the relationships she realized were important to her. She didn't want to delete them—they were valuable.

Deal with the Negatives

In the surveys, many women told me they learned that people pleasing is a waste of time, even though we all do it from time to time! So was perfectionism, worrying over doing things "right" versus doing the right things. Many wished they'd been more assertive. I heard the late Jean Lush, a noted counselor, say at a women's retreat, "I wish I hadn't been such a doormat!"

"My life's over, and I haven't lived it yet!" a midlife woman who'd married early in life said to me. She felt she'd given away huge chunks of her life and now didn't know how to reclaim it. Another woman tearfully told of her deep regret in marrying her husband—and the subsequent years of turmoil as they eventually divorced. Regrets can be painful, but there comes a time to let go of them. Regrets are such time wasters. There also is a time to realize that perhaps we can't have it all. Some women who have postponed children or have not married feel an intense longing, a sense of being unfulfilled. Then it's time to see with clear eyes what we do have and to develop it, use it. It's not always greener on the other side of the fence.

Sometimes as we do an inventory, we see mistakes we have made. It's time to let guilt go too and realize none of us is perfect. We all make mistakes.

To deal effectively with the present and the future, we need to ask clarifying questions. They help us to see the real issues at hand. The really important questions we dare to ask help us focus. I believe that is why this inventory was so emotional for some women. It helps us see the truth. It's important to ask empowering, big questions whenever we encounter a crossroads, so we will begin to see our lives with more clarity.

Last summer, we had forest fires raging all around us, one very near our home. The local authorities held a meeting and discussed evacuation routes. The fire ranger recommended we put what was most valuable in boxes, "just in case." We came home and put together a couple of boxes of essentials. There wasn't that much, really—it would fit into our car. I realized very few things are essential: Important papers. Pictures of our precious family. A few of our favorite books. Our computers. Maybe that's what the writer of Hebrews means when he says, "Our God is a consuming fire" (12:29 NIV), and the good stuff we want to keep is really quite simple.

It's time to realize that in spite of life's challenges (and oh, they never cease!), we can have a deep sense of God's faithfulness. It is like an underground, deep-flowing river that is always nourishing us. As we place our lives, and all that we have and are, in his hands, we will find joy in him.

Prayer

Lord, as I look at my life, I ask for courage to see what it is you have placed there and then to offer it willingly to you. I pledge my life, my all, to share your truth, whether through silent, intercessory prayer, ordinary acts of kindness, speaking, writing, service, or being a listening ear. If you can use anything, Lord, you can use me. May I have courage and initiative to grow and develop in new areas that I never thought possible. Renew my dreams, Lord, to be all that you would have me be, for your sake. In Jesus' name I pray this. Amen!

Mapping Your Next Step

Read the story in 2 Kings 4:1–7. Take time to discuss any insight you have from the passage and answer these questions:

- What material possessions do you have? Think about it: Do you possess them, or do they possess you?
- What talents and gifts do you possess?

MY PERSONAL INVENTORY

God does not want us to abandon those dreams (aspirations from God to develop and use our gifts for His purposes) . . . but will lovingly work with us
to refine our unrealistic dreams
to restore our broken dreams
to realize our delayed dreams, and
to redesign our shattered dreams
so that both His purposes and our dreams can be fulfilled.

David Seamands[5]

Find a quiet place to think with a notebook and pen. Write down all the things you are doing and all the things that are filling up your time.

Then cross off the things you should stop doing. (A clue: When you feel drained by something, it's a good indication you need to stop doing it. When you feel energized by something, it's an indication this might be something worth investing your time in.) Write down things you should add. Thoughtfully answer these questions:

- If my life were absolutely perfect, how would it look now?
- As I look back on my life, what am I glad I did?
- What things did I once do that I now consider a waste of time?
- Use answers to the previous questions to answer: Where should I now invest my time, energy, and money?
- Is there anything I should delete from my life?
- What person(s) made a difference in my life?
- How can I be that for someone else?

- What connections do you have, and how might they help you?
- What experiences have you had, and how can you use them?
- What dreams do you have? What steps might you take to further them?
- What things are cluttering your life that you need to delete? What would your life look like without them?

PART 2

Selah

Here we are, at this place in life. This junction: The empty-nest place. The fresh start after a divorce place. The brand-new vocation place. It may be the emptiness after a major personal loss, and it feels like a wondering place. Or can we call it a Selah time?

It's time to stop. To slow down and take a deep breath. Pay attention to where we are before we proceed.

It's time to step back to see, using the quilt metaphor, what kind of design we are making. It may take some thought, some input from others as we sort through our pieces of fabric, trying to decide what to keep, what to use. Sometimes we stand back and study the pieces, play with new arrangements.

We help the creative process along by watching and listening to others, those within our circle. One woman said, "We may not realize it, but often we are making quilts with the threads of advice we share with others."

So it is with our lives. We come to a time where we must critically look at the design we are making and wish to make. It's time for a Selah.

5

Time Out

Elijah:
Rest for the Rest of the Journey

> In our whole life melody the music is broken off here
> and there by rests, and we foolishly think we have
> come to the end of time. God sends a time of forced
> leisure, a time of sickness and disappointed plans, and
> makes a sudden pause in the hymns of our lives, and
> we lament that our voice must be silent and our part
> missing in the music which ever goes up to the ear of
> our Creator. Not without design does God write the
> music of our lives. . . . If we look up, God will beat
> the time for us.
>
> John Ruskin

I t's not easy being a mighty prophet of God. You don't
make a whole lot of friends when you're prophesying
against King Ahab and his queen too. But they deserved
it, leading God's people into such debauchery and idol
worship. How could they have forgotten the rich heritage

of their faith in the God of Abraham and Isaac and Jacob? But they did.

So Elijah had to give out a few thunderings here and there and pronounce a drought. The drought hurt some good people too, but Ahab needed a drastic lesson. Then there was that amazing showdown with 450 prophets of Baal and 400 prophets of Asherah, Jezebel's special prophets. One against 850! Pretty tough odds. But Elijah knew God would show up. And he sure did. The false prophets were going crazy, trying to get their gods to consume their sacrifice, but nothing happened. Then Elijah poured water on his sacrifice to drive home the point: God Almighty was still God. He called fire from heaven. God's power came down with such force that along with the water-soaked sacrifice, fire consumed even the wood and stones.

Then there was quite a move of God. The people repented, proclaimed their faith in God, and destroyed all of those false prophets. Elijah told Ahab rain was on the way and left in a hurry, before the rain could choke the road with mud, to get to Jezreel.

When Jezebel heard what Elijah did, the fearless prophet had a pressing need to get out of town. She vowed to kill him, and Elijah knew she meant it. What a strange time, running alone in the desert. He was exhausted and depressed.

After a day of running, he sat under a juniper tree and prayed to die. Well, he didn't die; he slept. "Then as he lay and slept under a broom tree, suddenly an angel touched him and said, 'Arise and eat. . . .' The angel of the LORD came back to him the second time, and touched him, and said, 'Arise and eat, because the journey is too great for you'" (1 Kings 19:5, 7).

It must have been a little humbling, the mighty prophet Elijah receiving orders to eat, drink, and sleep, as if he were a child. But he knew he needed it. Then what a strange time, running alone in the desert for forty days and forty nights. It was after he got to the mountains and spent a day and night in the cave that God asked him—twice—"What are you doing here, Elijah?" Elijah gave God his rehearsed speech on what a fantastic job he'd done, faithfully proclaiming the truth (by himself, he might add), and now Jezebel intended to kill him.

Then God gave Elijah a fresh mission: to anoint and invest in new leadership. In other words, it was time to delegate some authority to others. And he reminded Elijah that there were seven thousand people in the land who had not bowed their knees to Baal! Elijah went back to take up his calling once again, renewed and refreshed.

What We Can Learn from Elijah

Welcome to the Selah place: a pause, a time-out. Some of us gratefully, intentionally come to this place. Some of us are driven here, perhaps by an illness, a major loss, or an unexpected surgery. Some of us have a job change, or a stirring that it's time for a change in occupation. You may be having some physical problems, and you feel as if you're out of control, not yourself. Maybe you are experiencing the emptiness of your house as your children leave home. Or a major earthquake has hit your life: Your husband died, and all you'd planned together is gone. Perhaps you've experienced the shattering of divorce, the pain of being laid off, or the worries of caring for a chronically ill child.

It may be that your life just isn't working like it used to. Perhaps a career that once brought you satisfaction and fulfillment is now boring, has lost its challenge, or has just worn you out. Like Elijah, you've had a fabulous success, but now you are just plain tired and don't know where to go from here. For whatever reason, you know you need to get away, to hear from God. You need a time-out!

Take Time to Rest

Behold, You desire truth in the inward parts,
And in the hidden part You will make me to know wisdom.

Psalm 51:6

Mary took a time-out to listen to Jesus even though Martha wasn't happy about it. But Jesus affirmed Mary for her priority, which encourages me to believe he understands the unique nature of us women.

Do we ever need the time-out! We may not be like the mighty prophet Elijah in most ways, but we're human the way he was. We get used up and need restoring. And in the pause of our lives, we can be intentional about seeing that we are replenished for the rest of the journey. It is a prime place to hear from God, if we'll pay attention. The temptation is to ignore this place, keep going, fill the calendar, stay busy. But how essential it is to take time out in order to have significant growth in the next phase of life.

We need physical restoration at times, because life depletes us. Many of us are sleep deprived and feel the effects of stress. With deadlines and pressure, we can overuse our adrenaline, and our bodies then must desperately try to catch up to what we are calling them to do. Especially in midlife, we must be so many things to so many people. Some of us are caring for our elderly parents, our children, and our grandchildren, not to mention working, and some of us have very high-stress jobs. Some of us are struggling with the drudgery of a vocation that doesn't really fit, or we feel ready to start a family—but our husbands don't.

Often we don't realize (until we are forced to) how much we need to be replenished not only spiritually, emotionally, and mentally but physically too. How much we need to rest. God revived Elijah with good food, water, and sleep before he gave him a new assignment. Food, water, sleep: how basic, yet how necessary.

Is your body telling you that you need physical rest? You may be irritated, in pain, not at the top of your game, and yet you're going and going and going. And you think, *Sure, it would be wonderful to have a week or two at the sea or the mountains. But how can I do that? My life is just not conducive to rest right now.* Let me say that sometimes you can't afford not to take a break.

When I was pregnant with our fourth son, I was exhausted and had morning sickness all the time. Bill was pastor of a church, and we had a very limited income. He did something so wonderful for me: He sold his little prized pickup, and with the money, he surprised me with two tickets to Hawaii for a week. We absolutely could not afford it, and yet we could not afford not to go. Years later, as I look back, I remember that wonderful week when we slept, ate delicious fresh pineapple and papayas, and soaked in the sun. My morning sickness completely vanished, and that special time sustained me in the year ahead.

If there is any way possible, I urge you to make getting away to rest a priority. I have a friend who regularly schedules personal retreats at a convent. I love to get away and be with my husband, and we are due for another getaway soon, but there are times we need to be alone too. It can feel selfish, but if we constantly give out, we must be renewed. Whenever I am involved in a book writing project, I take several days to go by myself to a favorite place on the coast to think and write. While these are working vacations, they help replenish my spirit. I've noticed that nothing restores my husband physically like a fishing trip, especially to the ocean. He comes back with eyes shining (and usually fish)!

Give Yourself a Break

In order to go on to greater effectiveness, there are times when we must stop. After Elijah's retreat in the wilderness, he went back to life and began investing in others again. We need refreshing pauses because life is constantly changing, and we are too. Changes are not bad. They're just changes. When we reach midlife, occasionally we receive a wake-up call to remind us that we're changing. I was shocked one Tuesday when a clerk at Ross Dress for Less asked if I wanted the senior discount. Since my big birthday was a month away, I declined, but I confess I went home and immediately scheduled an appointment to have my hair colored. What? *Moi?* A senior-citizen discount?

The truth is, we are finite creatures. We get used up. Life takes it out of us, no matter where we are in life. When our sons were small, my husband would make a point of coming home from the office and giving me a day away from the house at least once every two weeks. He'd say, "Go shopping, go to the library, or go out to lunch." As much as I loved my little boys, how welcome those breaks were! I'd always come home ready to take them on again.

When I entered puberty, the changes were exciting, momentous. At about age fourteen, I heard someone describe the menstrual cycle rather romantically as the "womb weeping for its loss." I told my mother that my womb was now "weeping for its loss," and she said with her dry humor, "Well, it had better be!" But now as I enter the menopause phase, I realize why there's so much humor around menopause and the aging process. You have to laugh, or you'd cry.

The other day, I listened to a woman doctor on a morning talk show discuss menopause. She listed all of the symptoms with a gracious smile, and I ticked off my own as she went down the list. Bladder discomfort? Check. Lack of sexual drive? Check. Palpitations? Check. Vaginal dryness? Check. Weight gain? Check! On and on she went, with a weird, plastic smile that I found a little odd. When the program was over, I thought, *Well, where's the good news in all of this?*

The thing is, I really do believe there is good news. We could say some of the same things about pregnancy, about all the enormous changes that take place in a woman's body, but they eventually produce something wonderful. The changes of menopause also remind me that I am graduating to another place of life. Even all of the discomforts of menopause—the hot flashes, interrupted sleep, strange new aches and pains—are, in a way, birth pangs birthing a new phase of life that offers our greatest potential yet to fulfill some delayed promises.

The Selah place is an opportunity to rest, to become replenished. If you can't take an extended time (and rethink that, because if something is important, we make time for it), do some mini time-outs: an extended walk or a day at home when we ignore the to-do list. A friend of mine who is very influential in public speaking tells me that one day a month, she doesn't get dressed or answer the phone for the whole day. She takes a long soak in the tub and basically has a spa treatment at home: She gives herself a facial and a pedicure. She is one of the most giving and spiritual women I know, but she's learned the secret of physical restoration.

My wonderful son and daughter-in-law, Carly, gave me three gift certificates for massages this last year! After sitting at the computer and feeling the pressure of deadlines, I find a mini time-out so relaxing. I'm definitely a believer in therapeutic massage.

Find Fresh Perspective

Elijah had to get away to see his mission with new eyes. He'd been successful, but he had reached a crisis point. There was a big change in the country as well as in his personal life, as Jezebel was trying to kill him.

While nobody is trying to kill us, sometimes life can be threatening. It is so important to get away in order to gain new perspective. It will do wonders for you. We have some close friends who are extremely productive and giving, but last week they needed to get away, yet they didn't have an extended time to do that—only one day. They drove their RV to a river thirty miles away, and while it wasn't far from home, it was away from the phone and the scene of their many responsibilities, and it offered them a beautiful and different environment. They sat and enjoyed the sound of the rushing river; they took time to stop and rest.

If you have to wait an hour or two in an airport or at a shopping mall, you see people and things you didn't notice before. Until you actually sit down and look, you don't comprehend a lot of things around you. Sometimes nuances are subtle, and we need new eyes to be aware of the insights God has for us. Often in my writing, when I am stuck trying to express a concept, I put down my work and go for a walk. The change of scene helps me relax, and often the thought becomes clear. Betsy West, a friend who has many responsibilities in her church and community in the Washington, D.C., area, is taking a break this month by climbing Mount Kilimanjaro! I am eager to hear how it goes for her, because I know that this radical change in scenery will offer her new perspective and will be refreshing and stimulating.

A time-out helps you see what's worth treasuring, where you are, and maybe what needs to change. It also gives you perspective on what God has done in your life!

Frederick Buechner advises, "Listen to your life. See it for the fathomless mystery it is. In the boredom and pain of it no less than in the excitement and gladness; touch, taste, smell your way to the holy and hidden heart of it because in the last analysis all moments are key moments, and life itself is grace."[1]

Pace Yourself for the Journey

I love reading about the epic pioneer movement. Many of the families in wagon trains going west decided to observe the Sabbath, to take a day of rest. It was the Lord's Day, they reasoned, but it also helped them pace themselves for the journey. Their animals and children needed it as well. I believe we need to revisit the concept of keeping the Sabbath holy. I'm not talking about a rigid, legalistic observance of it, but there's wisdom in the concept of seasons for periodic time-outs in order to rest.

I speak at various women's retreats every year, and while they are inspiring, they can be very draining. I need to make sure I am refreshed and fed myself. I don't speak in the summer or in certain months in the winter, which helps me pace myself. It's important to schedule *unscheduled* time. The Eighty-fourth Psalm says that God provides springs and places of rest in the desert—oases—where, if we will look for them, we will find refreshment. We must periodically stop in order to go forward.

When you've been under mental and spiritual stress, doing something physical or creative helps bring balance: yard work, biking, playing the piano. Different people find different ways of restoring themselves physically. You know what works for you and what could be a mini time-out for you. Trying to make a craft would, quite frankly, drive me crazy. My husband, however, finds it restful to craft something in his workshop. Thomas á Kempis wrote these words of wisdom centuries ago: "So long as you wear this mortal body, you will be subject to weariness and sadness of heart. When this happens, you will be wise to resort to humble, exterior tasks, and to restore yourself by good works."[2]

My friend Gerry lives in Seattle and has recently retired from a demanding job in education. She says, "It's quite a transition going from achievement to appreciation, and it's harder than you might think. I'm finding a lot of my time is in looking out for my parents, husband, and step-children, and in making a good home for my family. I'm thinking this is a honeymoon period until I find my niche." This is a Selah time for her as she rests from her years of hard work and prepares for the future.

My husband and I were talking about this concept and how needed it is, no matter where we are in life. "I wish we could take a sabbatical," I said. He said, "Why can't we? Let's do it. Let's schedule one month next year."

I looked at him. "But—we've never done that before!"

"I know," he grinned. "That's why we need to do it." So we scheduled it. We're so excited; we can't wait!

Remember That God Is God

Maybe you're like me—you tend to worry. And there's never an end of things over which to worry. I'm learning that I can be concerned and pray, but most of life is beyond my control. There are times I must make a conscious decision to trust him, to remember that he is God.

The prophet Isaiah wrote:

Have you not known?
Have you not heard?
The everlasting God, the LORD,
The Creator of the ends of the earth,
Neither faints nor is weary.
His understanding is unsearchable.
He gives power to the weak,
And to those who have no might He increases strength.
Even the youths shall faint and be weary,
And the young men shall utterly fall.
But those who wait on the LORD
Shall renew their strength;
They shall mount up with wings like eagles,
They shall run and not be weary,
They shall walk and not faint.

Isaiah 40:28–31

The writer of Hebrews says, "There remains . . . a rest for the people of God" (Heb. 4:9). Jesus said, "Come to Me, all you who labor and are heavy laden, and I will give you rest" (Matt. 11:28). He calls us to come to him: to put down all that we have and are and simply let him hold us. The beautiful Twenty-third Psalm says that he leads us beside still waters; he restores our souls. Take a deep breath! God is in control.

I am sitting this very moment on my friend's deck, which overlooks a lake. It is a quiet early morning, and the waters are so still there is an almost perfect reflection of the trees on the opposite side of the lake. Earlier this morning, I put down my writing and walked to the lake and sat on the dock, just admiring the beauty. Still waters reflect. A time-out is an opportunity to reflect on the goodness and faithfulness of God, his never-failing mercy and love. As I sat, I just took in the beauty of that fact, along with the loveliness of the lake.

Reflecting on who he is gives me perspective on how to live. I can practice being still in my spirit and listening for the still, small voice, no matter where I am.

One summer I had a forced time-out. I had been diagnosed with lupus, but after four years of medication and other treatment, I learned I had fibromyalgia, probably caused by stress in my life. That summer, as family life went on as usual, I memorized Psalm 91 and tried to understand what it meant to abide under the shadow of the Almighty.

My normal, busy life as a mother and wife, and my other responsibilities with helping a magazine company, went on—but I had an almost parallel life, memorizing that passage, meditating on it in my walks and in my journal. It was a spiritual oasis for me, and an important part of my complete healing. I am grateful for health, and I've learned that our bodies, minds, and souls need rest.

Selah times are necessary, seasonal times and not places where we stay. The reflection, the pause from our busy lives, is a refueling spot. We live in a fearful world, ominous, really, if we look at the threat of terrorism, widespread epidemics, nations in turmoil. We need more than ever to know God, to hear his voice. I've found it feeds my soul to keep worship CDs in my car. Listening to good music and singing along gives me such a lift—a mini time-out that helps me focus on our faithful God. Andrew Murray wrote the following in 1895, and it speaks to us today.

How to Wait on God

Before you pray, bow quietly before God and seek to remember and realize who He is, how near He is, how certainly He can and will help.

Just be still before Him and allow His Holy Spirit to waken and stir up in your soul the childlike disposition of absolute dependence and confident expectation.

Wait upon God as a Living Being, as the Living God who notices you and is just longing to fill you with His salvation.

Wait on God till you know you have met Him; prayer will then become so different. . . . Let there be intervals of silence, reverent stillness of soul, in which you yield yourself to God, in case He may have aught He wishes to teach you or to work in you.

Waiting on Him will become the most blessed part of prayer, and the blessing thus obtained will be doubly precious as the fruit of such fellowship with the Holy One.[3]

So pause. Reflect. Think on what's important, not urgent. The pause helps you remember that we are not in control; he is.

Here is the truth: God has never failed us in the past; he won't fail us now. We can trust him. Waiting on God reminds us who our Source is—our Provision. There is none other! Believe for today, and you will believe for your future.

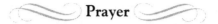
Prayer

Lord, I praise you that you call us to come away. Sometimes I'm driven to a time-out with you due to trauma or hurts. Lord, I want to come to you willingly and joyfully—in concentrated times and in other shorter times to reflect on my life in you. I need your restoration and nourishment. Help me to be a good steward of the life you've given me. In Jesus' name, amen.

Mapping Your Next Step

Read about Elijah's time-out in 1 Kings 18–19. How had Elijah's life changed in chapter 19?

- Why do you think he needed his time-out?
- Can you point to a time in your life where you especially needed to rest?
- In our very hectic lives, how can we take time-outs—mini ones as well as more extended ones?
- As you look at what is going on in your life right now, can you tell what God is saying to you?
- Perhaps you sense an emptiness in your life now, for whatever reason. In your prayer time, in your prayer journal, seek God for his creative touch on your life. Dare to dream a new dream for God. Why not say yes with all of your heart to what he has for you?

Idea

Why not have a Selah at your house for a day or an afternoon? If it's for just yourself, take the phone off the hook, relax, and try to "waste time" being with him.

Or invite in some friends and ask them all to bring a Scripture verse or short inspirational quote to share. Have food catered or everyone bring something. Laugh, cry, play, and pray. Be creative!

6

Ready and Waiting

The Ten Virgins:
Who's Foolish? Who's Wise?

Watch therefore, for you know neither the day nor
the hour in which the Son of Man is coming.

Matthew 25:13

It was going to be the wedding of the year. The bride and
groom were from well-respected families in the community, and all people could talk about for weeks was the
wedding. Finally it was time for the festivities to begin. It
started with a feast at the home of the bridegroom with his
groomsmen. As was the custom, the bride and her ten attendants waited near the bride's home. Tradition held that
the bridesmaids kept their lamps burning to light the way
for the groom's procession as it came to get the bride.

The bride's ten attendants were a close-knit group.
They'd grown up together, knew each others' dreams well,
and had shared many adventures. They were excited to

be part of the wedding party and had looked forward to it for a long time.

The night the wedding was to begin, the guys were taking a long time at their feast, and the girls were getting tired of waiting. It had been a long day, as they had worked hard at helping with the preparations, and now they were exhausted. And it seemed as if the groom was never going to show up. To try to stay awake, they sat in a little garden near the bride's home and chatted about the wedding: Who was going to be at the feast? What would be served?

They talked of their own plans and dreams for their weddings someday. It seems to be true that a groom plans for his wedding after he gets engaged; the bride plans her wedding from the time she is a little girl. After all, it's one of the biggest events in a woman's life. The thing about big moments, though, is that they are preceded by many small, boring ones: planning, details, details, and details until the big moment finally comes. The music starts to play, and then the real event happens. Until then, you wait and try to get ready.

Before long, the young women's conversation lulled as one by one, they fell asleep. Suddenly a cry sounded from down the street: "The bridegroom is coming!" The girls jumped up, scrambling to get ready. Five of the girls realized with dismay that the oil in their lamps was low, and they were about to run out. What could they do? "Can we borrow some from you?" they cried to their friends.

They could hear the approaching party, the laughter, the band beginning to play the music. The five girls who had planned ahead and brought extra oil were annoyed. "No, we can't give you ours or we won't have any. Why don't you go to the man who sells it and get your own?" The five girls left in a hurry to find an oil merchant. The other five joined the wedding party that was now beginning its celebration, and they all went into the courtyard for the joyous time. To keep thieves out, the door was locked behind them. Unfortunately, by the time the other girls got there with their newly purchased oil, the door was shut—and it was too late.

What We Can Learn from the Virgins

There is a lot to think about in this passage. If we look at the context in which Jesus told this story, he was talking about the end of the age, and what it means to live in readiness. Jesus reminds us in these provocative passages in Matthew 24–25, as well as in Luke 12, to be aware of the signs of his coming. He tells us to pay attention to the signs of the age, to watch. To be ready and waiting. All of the ten virgins were waiting, but only five were ready. And they were ready because they had enough oil.

Oil—it keeps our lamps burning in order to light the way. Near where I grew up in Montana there were oil wells, and I remember my uncle drilling for oil on his property, hoping to find reserves that would give him more resources. If you think about it, oil is a huge commodity in our whole world economy. Oil is vital reserved energy. I see prayer as our "oil"—our spiritual reserves—that helps us live in readiness as we wait in this Selah time.

We can only speculate why the five virgins missed out, but we can learn from their mistakes.

Plan Ahead

They didn't get enough oil because they didn't anticipate how long they would have to wait. As their wait extended, their oil got used up. Maybe they also naively assumed someone would give extra to them and didn't take personal responsibility to see that they had their own. Maybe they got bored and distracted. They may have lost hope that he was going to get there anytime soon and quit expecting him. Their faith went only so far—and then they ran out.

101

If they had prepared for the bridegroom's arrival, they would have participated in the wedding. Because they didn't, they missed it.

Ensure Sufficient Reserves

When the five foolish virgins discovered, to their dismay, that they'd run out, the five wise virgins told them to go get their own oil. Oil doesn't just show up on our doorsteps—there's an abundant supply available, but each person must get it for herself.

I wonder if there could be another reason too. Sometimes people who procrastinate are perfectionists—they put off a task because everything they put their hands to has to be done so well. Some perfectionists have trouble getting things done because they're waiting for the perfect time or place, which usually doesn't arrive. They can end up missing the event.

We can ensure sufficient reserves when we remember who supplies us with oil. When I was a young mother, I used to drop in to visit Grandma Ferlen, an eighty-nine-year-old woman in our community who, besides being a cute little old lady, had a powerful ministry of prayer. She intrigued me, and being with her was like having a conversation with both her and Jesus. She used to pick up and hug one of my children, pray a blessing over him or her, then turn to me, and continue our conversation.

She used to tell me, "Honey, this is my favorite verse: 'For I know whom I have believed, and am persuaded that he is able to keep that which I have committed unto him against that day!" (2 Tim. 1:12 KJV).

The oil reserves in her life were substantial; they overflowed, blessing so many around her, and they came out of knowing the Lord. She saw many answers to her prayers, and I thought, *I want what she has*. Later I realized how important it was for me to develop my own prayer life, one that would bear fruit. From watching Grandma Ferlen, I knew her Source—who could be mine too!

Get Yourself Some Praying Friends

> We exist for each other, and when we're at low ebb, sometimes just to see the goodness radiating from another can be all we need in order to rediscover it in ourselves.
>
> Kathleen Norris, *The Cloister Walk*

I privately call this "the girlfriend chapter," because it helps illustrate how women gather in groups—to talk, to work, to laugh. And to pray for one another. As my friend LeeAnn says, "Where would I be without my wonderful, dear friends?"

We learn a lot from each other, and we're not afraid to ask, "Where did you get those adorable shoes?" Or "Do you know anybody who gives a really good haircut?" Or "What are you doing about hot flashes?" I just haven't heard my husband and sons have conversations like this with their guy friends. We women share information with each other and are glad to give our sources.

General friends are wonderful resources, but there's something special about praying friends. Bill's mother tells me that when she was young—in the days when women ironed—her best friend used to come over with her ironing board and stacks of clothes, and they spent Tuesdays ironing, talking, and sharing prayer needs and answers.

You are blessed if you have a small-group prayer cell, or friends you can call who will support you in prayer. It is one of the greatest strengths you can have as you go through life. It takes constant cultivating to have praying friends, and to be one. As my life has changed over the years, my prayer groups have changed somewhat, even though my dearest friends remain constant, and I know I can still

103

phone them for prayer. Some of my friends and I exchange prayer needs via e-mail.

I am also in a Bible study group that means the world to me. Though I'm a delinquent member because I'm gone a lot, I do my best to make it a priority when I'm in town.

The group's relationships have deepened in the last two years as we have studied the Bible together and prayed for each other. We have seen some amazing answers to prayer. I also have a smaller prayer cell with four other women, and the strength of their prayers is an indescribable treasure and force. Praying friends—how we need them!

Remind Each Other Where to Get the Oil

Women who have their lamps filled with oil and are ready in season and out to share encouragement from God, and who are willing to pray—I find them in the most unexpected places. Earlier this spring I was scheduled to speak in Oklahoma City. Before I left on the trip, I sensed an overwhelming need for prayer. I e-mailed my prayer group, shamelessly begging them to pray that my speaking would lift up Jesus' name. On my flight there, I was one of three women in a row, and I had the aisle seat. I pulled out *My Utmost for His Highest,* and the woman next to me exclaimed, "Oh, that's my favorite devotional!"

She told me she was a Christian and had a counseling practice. The younger woman in the window seat, who had been studying a textbook (she was on her way to take a final exam for her master's degree in speech pathology), put down her reading and joined in. She was a Christian too.

Before we landed, all three of us joined hands twice to pray for each other in our various needs, and I got off the plane, grateful for the prayer, surprised once more at the instant bond in knowing Jesus.

I might have known God was about to do something extraordinary. The next evening when I spoke, twelve hundred women were in attendance, which astounded me because I thought they might cancel due to tornado warnings. But the incredible Oklahomans seemed to take it all in stride. One woman told me, "Not to worry—the tornado's on the other side of the freeway!" I suppose it would be like Montanans canceling a conference due to a snow prediction, or Oregonians canceling due to rain.

After I finished speaking, the tornado warning siren went off, and many of us were hustled to the center of the large church, then into a smaller auditorium that doubled as a choir room and storm shelter. "Get down, get down," the leaders said as they hurried us in and shut the door. I confess to being very wide-eyed about the whole thing. Then the real event began.

Many of the women had their cell phones, and their husbands or family members called, telling them where the tornado was. We began a spontaneous prayer service, interceding for people in different areas where the threat seemed to be greatest. A woman went to the piano, and we sang songs like "He hideth my soul in the cleft of the rock." Some women stood to quote passages of Scripture. An older woman who leads a group called the Anna Women led us in prayers. I found out later the Anna group in this state-wide women's ministry consists of older women devoted to prayer. How appropriate was her leadership!

Then a younger woman with long, dark hair stood, her voice breaking with emotion and passion. "We are praying for the physical safety of our children," she said, "and we must. But I believe God is reminding us of the spiritual darkness and danger of our world, and we must pray for the *spiritual* safety of our children. And not only our children but people everywhere! He is not willing that any should perish!"

My eyes fill with tears even now as I think of it, because she symbolized to me a woman standing in the gap,
praying for her generation, holding the forces of darkness
back from touching her family. We had a powerful prayer
meeting, unlike any I've been to for a long time. We didn't
talk about prayer; we didn't get philosophical about prayer;
we prayed.

The storm passed; the women went home; I went to
my hotel.

The next day, my hostess told me that her home church
had been destroyed that night, but the people had been
planning to rebuild anyway and were making the best of
it. They amazed me with their strength—maybe it came
from their having survived the storms of the Dust Bowl,
the Great Depression, and more recently, the bombing of
the federal building in their city. The occasional storms
just made them dig down deep to their Source.

Storms? Sure. But Jesus is still Lord. And he is coming
soon, and we must be ready. We can think, "Oh, people
have talked about Jesus coming back for so long, obviously
it's not going to happen very soon." So we fall asleep. But I
believe that God is calling us to prayer for really big needs
in our world, our nation, our families, and our communities. And I need prayer in my very real life, just as you do.
I call frequently on my friends, and I believe their prayer
bears fruit. They are praying for me this very day, as I am
working on this book, and I'm humbly grateful for the
intercessions of these spiritual midwives! I have a list of
some of their prayer needs, and I am praying for them too.
(By the way, the best way to get some praying friends is to
be one yourself.)

This powerful ministry of praying for one another has
a mysterious and amazing quality: The reserves don't run
out as long as we keep going to the Source. If we set our
eyes on the challenges or needs that face us, we can be
overwhelmed. Like the five foolish virgins, we might simply

run out of energy and say, "It's no use!" But we can choose to keep our eyes on Jesus and trust him to replenish our reserves so that we will be ready for whatever adventure and challenge he may show us.

Fill Your Own Lamp

What is the greatest power of my life? Is it work, service, sacrifice for others, or trying to work for God? The thing that ought to exert the greatest power in my life is the Atonement of the Lord. It is not the thing we spend the most time on that moulds us the most; the greatest element is the thing that exerts the most power.

Oswald Chambers

We must get our own oil for our lamps. It's not enough to live on our mothers' or husbands' faith or just show up in church. It's not even enough to hang out with friends who have active prayer lives. We get our own oil from developing our own relationship with Jesus Christ on an ongoing basis. We become ready through the nonglamorous basics that we all know yet find easy to neglect: reading his Word prayerfully, asking him to show us what we are to learn from him. We become ready in finding quiet moments simply to ask the Lord to fill us with his Holy Spirit. It's such a daily thing. And it needs to be, because as we go through each day, we do use up the oil!

Being ready is a consequence of prayer. A life of prayer means simply having a constant conversation with God as we go through our ordinary, daily tasks. It's possible to do the necessary things we are called to do yet keep an inner eye waiting and watching. It's easy to get caught up in the mundane—especially when our hands are full with our First Calling.

But the joy of the Selah place is that we have an opportunity now to stand back and see the real issues at hand and to pray for God's will to be done.

I think about the great women of prayer who have so instructed me by their lives:

- Evelyn Christenson, who wrote *What Happens When Women Pray* and is still an influence in prayer movements in America and around the world.
- Catherine Marshall and her ministry of intercession. Catherine has gone to be with the Lord, but her books and passion for God have influenced countless people.
- My mother.
- My eighty-two-year-old friend Dorothy Book, who still prays faithfully for so many.
- My eighty-two-year-old mother-in-law, Betty Carmichael, who prays every night for her large extended family.

You most likely have them in your life—women who live in spiritual readiness. And now we are in the place where we see it's time for us to step up to the plate, to pray for the needs in the lives of those around us—to take our places to pray for our children, our grandchildren. This is what we at the Selah place are being called to: the life of prayer.

We can get so earthbound! Someone gave me a little plaque for my office that shows an old woman and bears the inscription, "I've grown old waiting for you." Are we growing old waiting for Jesus, or do we anticipate his coming with joyful expectation? The prophetess Anna, the elderly woman who prayed in the temple, did not stop looking for the Messiah. And one day Joseph and Mary came with baby Jesus—the Messiah! And she saw him!

Your Invitation to the Wedding

Be ready in season and out of season.

2 Timothy 4:2

In a few months, our son Christian is marrying Jami. Another family wedding, and we are excited. It was only a year ago this week that our son Eric married Carly, and what a great time that was. Chris and Jami's upcoming wedding will mean several days of celebration too: showers, rehearsal dinner, the wedding itself, the reception, and the next day, a family reunion. These events take planning. Already we are making lists (Jami's mother more than I, as Jami is her only daughter, and she's pulling out all the stops!).

As we make our lists, we are trying to anticipate anything unexpected. So far, we have booked the church, the reception location, the restaurant for the rehearsal dinner. We are planning accommodations for the dozens of out-of-town relatives. Aunt Kitty is catering the wedding reception, and we have chosen the menu. Before the actual wedding, we will buy the necessary goods, then begin another level of preparation.

Since we really believe this wedding is going to take place, we have taken concrete steps. Chris has bought the ring; Jami has her dress. We are getting ready! It's not a halfhearted preparation; it's intentional, getting ready with confidence. We can imagine the day: It will be a beautiful September late afternoon. The wedding guests are seated in the church, listening to strains of "Jesu, Joy of Man's Desiring." Chris and his brothers, and Bill and Uncle Bob, who will officiate at the ceremony, are at the front of the church in a side room, waiting. Jami is in the bride's room at the back of the church, her bridesmaids gathered around her as they put on the finishing touches. Her mother kisses her, her eyes filled with tears, her heart full of love and joy. The mother of the groom is out front with Grandma and Grandpa Carmichael, who walk a bit slower but are beautiful nonetheless in their age and years. We treasure the old ones so!

The wedding party begins its procession, with first the tanned and glowing bridesmaids—Jami's sisters and Chris's little sister, Amy, all quite elegant in black as they come down the aisle to meet the handsome groomsmen. Six-year-old Willy and three-year-old Kendsy, now quite the professionals at being ring bearer and flower girl, begin walking down the aisle before the bride, and everyone smiles and laughs. They are so gorgeous! There is something fresh and beautiful about children in a wedding party—even their unexpected little side trips. It reminds us of the hopefulness and possibilities of marriage.

There's a pause in the music. Chris comes out the side door with his father and Uncle Bob, along with his three brothers and close friends. Chris's eyes are at the back of the church, which tells us she is there! The bride is ready, exquisite in a shimmering ivory dress. The dramatic wedding march begins as everyone stands to see beautiful Jami, holding her father's arm as they walk to the front of the church. Chris and Jami are radiant—all the planning and anticipation are now past, and this is their moment.

Although the day is not here yet, I am anticipating this wonderful celebration for our family. And although the great and glorious day of the Lord is not here yet, and I do not know all of the plans he has for me in the second phase of my life, until he comes, I can dream. I can plan. I can prepare! I can keep my lamp filled with oil and be ready.

Expect! Believe! Watch!

Sometimes the wait seems forever. We've waited, and we've prayed . . . and we are still waiting. We've asked the Lord to fill a certain need, and yet here we are still. We've prayed for direction, sensing deep inside that he does have a plan for us, yet we still wait for the doors to open. This is not an idle waiting; it's active, as we expand our borders to dream big dreams for God.

As you wait and pray, take any steps you feel God is leading you to take. Maybe it's further education to prepare yourself for the next thing God has for you. Maybe it's making a commitment to a prayer group a priority in your life, which will help develop the power of intercession in your life. It may mean putting legs to your prayers to plan and invest in the next phase of your life. Prayerfully set short-term and long-term goals, then make lists in order to accomplish them.

When we ask for prayer for ourselves, and faithfully pray for others, we can be sure of one thing: He is the Source for all of us, and his mercies never fail.

Prayer

Come, Holy Spirit, into every aspect, every season of my life. In this time of waiting, may I become a woman of prayer. Help me to open my eyes to the needs around me, to sense the urgency of the times to share your love with the lost. Fill me up, Lord. Life can drain the expectation and sense of anticipation of what you have in store for me. Through the power of prayer, may I catch a fresh vision of what it means to be ready as I wait for you. Amen.

Mapping Your Next Step

Prayerfully read the parable of the ten virgins in Matthew 25:1–13. Like Mary, treasure the words of this passage in your heart for a time—dwell on them, brood on them. Then answer:

- What does this parable say to you about human nature?
- Have you ever run out of something essential? What did you do to remedy the situation?
- Has someone's prayer life influenced you? How might you begin to be that person for someone else?
- Read 1 Thessalonians 4:11–18. Verses 11–12 discuss the value of leading a quiet life, minding our own business, working with our hands—then Scripture goes on to describe the dramatic events of Jesus' return. What does this say about how to live as we wait for him?
- How can you practically apply these principles to your own life?
- Verse 18 says, "Comfort one another with these words." How does talking about Christ's coming comfort us?

Idea

Ask two or three friends to join you in becoming a prayer group. Agree to meet monthly (or more, if possible). Make sure everyone has a small notebook in which to write each other's prayer needs and to record answers. Stress to everyone in the group that they must keep prayer needs confidential. Watch for God's response!

7

Delayed Dreams

Sarah:
From Barren Princess to Mother of Nations

> By faith Sarah herself also received strength to con-
> ceive seed, and she bore a child when she was past
> the age, because she judged Him faithful who had
> promised.
>
> Hebrews 11:11

S arah leaned on a large cushion and watched her handsome son, Isaac, with his father. Nothing gave her as
much pleasure as to stand back where she could look, un-
observed, at her two wonderful men. They were sitting on
the carpeted tent floor, having their meal. Isaac was ani-
mated, gesturing and laughing occasionally as he explained
something to his father. White-haired Abraham sat quietly,
but his eyes gleamed brightly with love and interest as he
nodded thoughtfully at some point Isaac was making.

How faithful God is, Sarah thought. If you had told her
twenty-seven years ago that she would give birth to a son,

she would have laughed in your face! Actually, she did laugh. She—with Abraham—give birth to a son at her age? Impossible!

But back to the beginning. Sarah was a blessed woman to be married to Abraham, a great, kind, and faithful man. When they started out their life together in Ur, their names were Sarai and Abram. Sarai meant "princess," and she was indeed every inch a princess—tall and elegant with an unforgettable mystique. People asked, "Who is she?"

Her existence was a nomadic one, as she followed her husband, who was developing an intimate (and somewhat awesome and frightening) relationship with Yahweh, almighty God. God had given them a big promise: that he would establish a mighty nation out of Abram and Sarai; that their seed would be like the sands of the sea. It was a lovely idea, but as the months and years went by, they received no sons. No daughters, either. Sarai was keenly aware of the rules: Women bore little importance until they gave their husbands sons, because it was through a son that a man lived on. Sarai was barren.

Over time, the couple gained wealth and influence, but they saw no sign of the promised offspring. Abram never said anything to Sarai, but the emptiness between them was palpable. After much thought, Sarai made the gesture: "Abram, take my handmaiden, Hagar—her son will be ours." That was the custom then; the handmaiden's child became the owner's. Hagar did become pregnant, but the relationship between Sarai and Hagar, once respectful and easy, became strained.

None of this turned out the way Sarai thought it would. Her charmed and beautiful life felt hollow. Hagar, proud to be pregnant with Abram's child, developed an attitude, and her mere presence caused Sarai such pain that she drove the pregnant and weeping Hagar out of their camp. But God intervened and met Hagar in the desert, and he sent her back to Abram. Ishmael was born, so Abram did have a son. *But he's not mine*, Sarai thought bitterly, as she watched the little boy playing. *Not mine.*

By this time God had changed their names to Abraham and Sarah. Little by little, he tested them, and they occasionally built altars, gradually understanding the covenant God was establishing with them. One day three mysterious visitors came with the word from God that Sarah was going to bear a son. At her age! Of course she laughed! Who wouldn't?

Yet it happened just as they said. A miracle! Sarah gave birth to Isaac, whose name means "laughter." From then on, Sarah's whole purpose and focus was Isaac, and a fierce sense of protection arose from somewhere deep inside of her. At Isaac's weaning party, she saw Ishmael teasing his little half brother. Maybe it was out of jealousy, because Isaac was getting a lot of attention. But that's when Sarah knew that Abraham must banish Hagar and Ishmael from the family. It was painful for many, but Isaac's inheritance had to be protected.

Now as Sarah, quite old and frail, watched Isaac and Abraham, she reflected on her life: how she started out with such high hopes, having married well. But then there was the unfolding disappointment in the intervening long, empty years of waiting for a son. She thought of the mistakes she'd made—insisting that Hagar produce a son for them, and the mess that followed. But God kept pursuing them, leading them, and they tried to follow, even though they made mistakes.

What meant the most to her was having God change her name from Sarai, meaning "princess," to Sarah, "mother of nations." She'd privately liked *Sarai* before the long years of childlessness. But what good is a princess if she's barren? How incredibly fulfilling it was, and what a surprise that after all this time, after all her errors in judgment, that God would trust her with a new definition, a new name, and a new purpose!

You shall be called by a new name,
Which the mouth of the LORD will name.
You shall also be a crown of glory
In the hand of the LORD,
And a royal diadem in the hand of your God.
You shall no longer be termed Forsaken,
Nor shall your land any more be termed Desolate;
But you shall be called ["My Delight Is in Her"].

Isaiah 62:2–4

What We Can Learn from Sarah

Define Yourself Accurately

Before God changed Sarah's name, it's quite possible her defining quality in her own mind was "beautiful but barren."

Some of our definitions are obvious; some negative ones we accept based on abuse, an enormous disappointment, or a tragedy. We privately hold some of our definitions; they are buried within us, and we whisper them only to ourselves and never admit them aloud: *Learning disabled. Second class. Stupid. Fat. No talent.*

Some of us are blessed to have a strong concept of who we are, and our biggest challenge is to overcome a happy life! But probably most of us fall into the category I consider myself to be in, that of having conflicting definitions. We developed these when we were offered both negative and positive input while we were young and impressionable, and we must consciously choose and rehearse the positive. Dr. Phil McGraw puts its well: "The past reaches into the present and programs the future by your recollections and your internal rhetoric about what you perceived to have happened in your life."[1]

My friend Lupe Dobbs is ten years younger than I am, but she has experienced a lot. She grew up in the fast life of Southern California and got into drugs and alcohol at an early age. Although she married and had children, alcohol shredded her hopes and dreams, and her life rapidly spiraled downward.

One day she was in county jail when two women arrived to teach a Bible study. For the first time, Lupe realized there was a way out for her, and Jesus was the way. She asked him into her life, and he radically transformed her. After she got out of jail, alcohol abuse threatened to snare her again. She and her husband realized they needed to make a major change to get away from negative influences around them, so they moved their family to Oregon.

Lupe went to church one Sunday, and the teacher of the class happened to be one of my dearest friends, June Curtis. June's background is different from Lupe's; in fact, June's husband is an attorney and judge. But June, entering the Second Calling and watching for opportunities to invest in people, recognized in Lupe a gifted, intelligent woman with a strong desire to grow past her problems. June saw that Lupe was passionate about sharing Jesus and his saving power with others.

June and Lupe became close friends. With June's constant encouragement, Lupe finished her undergraduate degree.

Tragically, Lupe's husband, Charles, died, leaving Lupe a young single mother. Lupe grieved, but she didn't give up. While working, she earned her master's degree to further train for ministry. She now pastors a church that reaches many who are now where Lupe was years ago.

I've been privileged to share ministry outreaches with Lupe, and she is a dynamic speaker. Not long ago, when she was ill, she told me how difficult it was when a health professional made a racially insensitive remark to her. She said with tears, "Her comment triggered that old definition of me: *alcoholic Hispanic from South Central L.A.!*"

But she was adamant: "That is not who I am! I'm a follower of Jesus Christ, and through his power I have over-

come my addictions. I've finished two degrees. I'm supporting my family, and God has a good plan for my life!"

Lupe has had to be proactive about not believing the
old definition of herself.

It is beautiful to see how God has led her and continues
to mold her as she helps so many whose lives have been
destroyed by alcohol and drugs.

Belief is a powerful thing and we must, like Sarah and
Lupe, believe God has something better for us. We must
accept his definitions of us.

Follow the Leader

> Blessed is the man whose strength is in You,
> Whose heart is set on pilgrimage.
>
> Psalm 84:5

Our hearts can be set on pilgrimage. This may seem like an
oxymoron, to be "set" on movement, on traveling. And yet,
that is truly what we are: pilgrims journeying through this
life. We either journey willingly, with a sense of adventure,
or complain and sigh the whole way. If you've ever traveled
with a group on an extended trip, you see that some people
are better travelers than others. The travelers you want to
be with are good sports who can roll with the punches and
see each day as an adventure.

Then there are those other dear people who have a hard
time leaving their comfort zones. They are more difficult
fellow travelers. Some of us may even be like the reluctant
pioneer woman I read about, who decided halfway through
the journey west that she was not going a step farther. As
the wagon train pulled out, to show her husband she was
serious about not moving on, she set fire to her wagon.
Finally her embarrassed husband physically picked her up,
threw her over his horse, and they galloped onward.

Abraham didn't have to do that with Sarah; she willingly followed him to new places for better grazing, followed God as he led them closer to the Promised Land. As they journeyed toward Canaan, they made altars at different places.

The principle we can learn from Sarah is that life changes constantly and that it is good to keep our hearts and minds set on following God through all of the twists and turns. When we have an attitude of *What wonderful adventure is next?* instead of *Oh dear, how am I going to handle this?* it makes such a difference in our lives—and in the lives of those who have to live with us!

It's as Oswald Chambers says in *My Utmost for His Highest:* "We grow spiritually by obeying God through the words of Jesus being made spirit and life to us, and by paying attention to where we are, not to whether we are growing or not. We grow spiritually as our Lord grew physically, by a life of simple, unobtrusive obedience."[2]

Keep Growing

Peter tells us, "Grow in the grace and knowledge of our Lord and Savior Jesus Christ" (2 Peter 3:18 NIV). When our hearts are set on pilgrimage, we are better prepared to grow from life's experiences. Life is basically a test. And it does seem that we learn and grow through the hardest things that come our way—through disappointments, and sometimes what seems interminable waiting. Sarah and Abraham learned from their hard times.

In your life experiences, what are some of the things you have learned? No doubt you learned through struggles, through difficulty, maybe through mistakes you have made. But the great thing is, you have more wisdom, more knowledge now that you can pass on to others. Douglas Steere wrote, "Saints . . . are ordinary people attending to the highest truth they know and are prepared to let this truth have undivided sway in their lives. [They] are not afraid of consequences because they are such avid lovers of the truth they have found."[3]

Sarah had some prime opportunities to grow. Abraham let her down when he lied to Pharaoh and told him she was his sister, not his wife. Abraham was the very one who should have protected her. No doubt she had to do some forgiving. And then she learned a profound lesson about what it means to wait for God's timing, through trying to force the issue of having a son by using Hagar. But she did learn. She kept learning, kept growing, and she is listed in the Hall of Fame chapter of Hebrews 11 as a woman of great faith.

If anything is certain, it is that every one of life's trials, if only because it breaks the hard crust of our physical and mental habits, creates an empty space where seed can be sown. "In the sudden void caused by a bereavement," Paul Tournier writes in *Creative Suffering,* "an illness, failure, loneliness—your mind is assailed by fundamental questions to which you hardly ever gave a thought in the coercive whirl of life."[4]

Wait for God's Timing

"For My thoughts are not your thoughts, nor are your ways My ways," says the LORD. "For as the heavens are higher than the earth, so are My ways higher than your ways, and My thoughts than your thoughts."

Isaiah 55:8–9

Sometimes we mistakenly believe God's timing will always be convenient for us and work into our schedule. Ask my friend Christine if that is so! She and her husband visited a Liberian orphanage to photograph children for a missions newsletter. God literally dropped a daughter into their laps, whom they eventually adopted, and Amma is now their fourth child. They were not looking for another daughter. Christine was just developing herself as an artist. Yet she will tell you it was God's timing, and it was right.

Sometimes God's timing seems very off. Sarah certainly didn't plan such a long wait for a child. I mentioned earlier that my good friend Ruth Lovegren and her husband, Ken, worked hard running a resort on a beautiful lake near here for many years. Their work was satisfying but confining, and they looked forward to traveling and enjoying retirement. The ink was barely dry on the sale of their resort when Ken, who seemed to be in good health, died unexpectedly and suddenly of a heart attack. Ruth discovered a few days later that he'd planned a surprise trip to Hawaii to celebrate the beginning of their retirement. Ken's death was a devastating loss for Ruth. She wondered, *Why did God take Ken now?*

Other situations can crop up in life that do not fit our overall plans. Perhaps you must work at a job that you don't enjoy, and you wonder, *Why must I take this job at this time in my life? Why can't I find some work that will pay better?*

Or maybe you're still waiting for that special man to complete your life, and you ask God: "Where is that wonderful husband you promised to send me?"

It's impossible to understand God's timing in our lives, but the bottom line is, we must trust that God is sovereign and his timing is perfect.

As my friend Ruth worked through her loss, she held on to this verse: " 'For I know the plans I have for you,' declares the LORD, 'plans to prosper you and not to harm you, plans to give you hope and a future' " (Jer. 29:11 NIV). God indeed has blessed Ruth and given her a different plan—one that makes her an inspiration to many.

God had a different plan for Sarah's life as well, but it was good.

God Is Your True Home

> LORD, You have been our dwelling place in all
>   generations.
> Before the mountains were brought forth,
> Or ever You had formed the earth and the world,
> Even from everlasting to everlasting, You are God.
>
> Psalm 90:1–2

One sunny Sunday afternoon two weeks ago, Bill and I decided to go for a walk. The war in Iraq was in full swing. There was loss of life and uncertainty how it would all turn out. Old hatreds and scores of various sects seemed impossible to solve. And all this was happening in the land where our faith began—where Abraham and Sarah started their lives together in Ur, near Babylon (which is now Baghdad). We took our Bible and went to the Mount Jefferson trailhead.

Along a rushing creek filled with fresh snowmelt grew some towering, old-growth Douglas firs. We stopped to stare at them in awe. On the other side of the trail were lava flows, and we reasoned that because of the creek and the lava, the trees had escaped the occasional forest fire.

We sat down on some rocks, talked about our nation, and prayed for our troops. We thought about how long those trees had been there—and how they were probably older than our country. The trees simply grew, their roots going deep, through the Civil War, World Wars I and II, the Korean War, the Vietnam War, the Gulf War . . . and now the Iraq War. Oblivious to all of it, the trees simply grew in their lovely spot, season after season.

There's a lesson here, I thought. It matters not what circumstances we are facing. God is faithful, no matter what. He is God, no matter what. When we put our roots down into him, just as the tree puts down its roots into the river, we can rest in him. It's a matter of trust.

The deep-flowing river speaks to me of God's faithfulness that is continuous, ever flowing, regardless of the changes and challenges of life. You would not want to change the flow of the river, to stop it, or even to analyze it. Instead, you sit beside it and enjoy it as you bask in its sound. We can do that with God's faithfulness: In spite of changes, in spite of loss, we can have a deep, settled security that he is our eternal home. We rest in knowing that he is a faithful God, and we are his works in progress.

Revisit Your Dreams

Go for your dreams! My husband has observed that many of his friends have changed careers three or four times in their lifetime. Don't be afraid to tend to your dreams—even long-delayed ones. As long as we live, we can learn and grow. A friend e-mailed me this inspiring story from an unknown author:

> The first day of school, our professor introduced himself and challenged us to get to know someone we hadn't already met. I was standing up, looking around, when a gentle hand touched my shoulder. I turned around to find a wrinkled little old lady beaming up at me with a smile that lit her entire being. She said, "Hi, handsome. My name is Rose. I'm eighty-seven years old. Can I give you a hug?" I laughed and enthusiastically responded. "Of course you may!" and she gave me a giant squeeze.
>
> "Why are you in college at such a young, innocent age?" I asked. She jokingly replied, "I'm here to meet a rich husband, get married, have a couple of kids."
>
> "No, seriously," I said. I was curious what motivated her to take on this challenge at her age.
>
> "I always dreamed of having a college education, and now I'm getting one!" she told me. After class, we walked to the student union building and shared a chocolate milkshake. We became instant friends. Every day for the next

three months, we left class together and talked nonstop. I was always mesmerized, listening to this "time machine" as she shared her wisdom and experience with me.

Over the course of the year, Rose became a campus icon, and she easily made friends wherever she went. She loved to dress up and reveled in the attention other students bestowed upon her. She was living it up.

At the end of the semester, we invited Rose to speak at our football banquet. She agreed. At the banquet, she cleared her throat and began, "We do not stop playing because we are old. We grow old because we stop playing. There are only four secrets to staying young, being happy, and achieving success.

- First, you have to laugh and find humor every day.
- Second, you've got to have a dream. When you lose your dreams, you die. There are so many people walking around who are dead and don't even know it!
- Third, understand the huge difference between growing older and growing up. If you are nineteen years old and lie in bed for one full year, not doing one productive thing, you will turn twenty years old. If I stay in bed for a year and never do anything, I will turn eighty-eight. Anybody can grow older. That doesn't take any talent or ability. The idea is to grow up by finding the opportunity in change.
- Fourth, have no regrets. The elderly usually don't have regrets for what they did, but rather for things they did not do. The only people who fear death are those with regrets."

At the year's end, Rose finished the college degree she had begun many years ago. One week after graduation, Rose died peacefully in her sleep. More than two thousand college students attended her funeral in tribute to the wonderful woman who taught by example that it's never too late to be all you can possibly be.

There's an old saying that has an important truth: "Believe your beliefs and doubt your doubts." When we put our roots down deep and trust God, we can have confidence that our lives will bear fruit . . . even if it seems that sometimes we must wait.

The prophet Jeremiah wrote, "Blessed is the man who trusts in the LORD, and whose hope is in the LORD. For he shall be like a tree planted by the waters, which spreads out its roots by the river, and will not fear when heat comes; but its leaf will be green, and will not be anxious in the year of drought, nor will cease from yielding fruit" (Jer. 17:7–8).

Accept a New Definition of You

Sometimes we get stuck thinking, *This is my lot in life. This is just who I am.* We might be tempted to think we will never fulfill the original promise that God had for us. Like Sarah, we may have tried to make it happen in our own way and timing, which only complicated matters and life, then became a huge mess. Or something unexpected happened to crush our dreams, and we've resigned ourselves to what is instead of anticipating what can be. We quit believing in the promise of our lives. So we stay with our old definitions, our old names.

My mother always had a fun-loving personality, true to her red hair and vaudeville background, but her laughter hid the pain of lost love and betrayal. When she met Jesus in her twenties, she was already a single mother and more than ready for God to write a new name for her. But in God's good timing, she met and married my father, who moved her and my older sister out to the ranch in Montana, and then she and my father went on to have six more children.

In some ways, my mother's life was like Sarah's—someone she trusted let her down; she waited for what seemed forever for God to fulfill his promise to her. But we, her children, witnessed the faithfulness of God written upon our mother's entire life. The day after my mother died, my sister Judy wrote the following poem, and I include it here with her permission. (Note: The last part of the final stanza is paraphrased from Hebrews 12:13 in the Living Bible.)

She Moves in Gentle Graces . . .

She moves in gentle graces through the day
Evoking memories of the early morn—
scent of lilac, and of coffee—
Family love and bustle—
adventure, fun and learning.

The heat of noonday sun beats down—
In memory's eye.
Dry-baked earth, and dusty field.
Strain and conflict—
grievous hurts and healing.

When afternoon comes stealing in
with stealthy shadow fingers
The godly wisdom of this Sarah
Comes like hyacinth, or Jasmine,
With growth and rediscovery.

Undaunted by the night outside
She clings securely to her Rock,
The calm of peace in midst of torrents
Joy dispelling speechless rage.

She moves in gentle graces through the day,
I see her "marking out with careful steps
That smooth straight path
So all who follow her,
Tho' some are weak and lame
Will become strong."[5]

Judy Volta

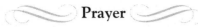

Prayer

Lord, give me fresh eyes to appreciate what can happen through the changes and tests of my life. I pray that you will give me once again the faith of a child to trust you for good things! Thank you for reminding me that I am precious in your sight, and that you do indeed have a good plan for me. Help me to enjoy the journey with you, Lord, and to see it as an adventure, not an endurance contest. Thank you for reminding me to dig down deep to know you in a fresh way . . . to trust you and your perfect timing. In Christ's name, amen.

Mapping Your Next Step

Read the story of Sarah in Genesis 11:29–23:2; also see Hebrews 11:11.

- How do you think Sarah changed over the years?
- As you look back over your life, what do you believe is your defining quality?
- What early messages influenced your self-image?
- Have you ever had to wait for something? If so, what did you learn about God's timing?
- Do you believe you have fulfilled the promise of your life yet?
- If not, what steps can you make in order to realize your dream?
- What inward change in thinking can help you make some needed outward changes?

8

In Love Again

Water to Wine:
Renewed Passion for Life

> My beloved spoke, and said to me: "Rise up, my love,
> my fair one, and come away. For lo, the winter is past,
> the rain is over and gone. The flowers appear on the
> earth; The time of singing has come, and the voice
> of the turtledove is heard in our land. . . . Rise up,
> my love, my fair one, and come away!"
>
> Song of Solomon 2:10, 13

Mary was looking forward to going to the wedding in Cana, because the bride was the daughter of some of her dearest friends. She couldn't help being reminded of the wonderful years she'd had with Joseph, their close family, and especially her extraordinary Son, Jesus. *How Joseph would have loved seeing everyone*, she thought. Sadly, he'd been gone for several years now. When Mary arrived at the wedding, she was glad to see many of their friends and family members.

Jesus had been invited to the wedding too, and he was there with his disciples. Mary was so pleased to see him. She sensed from watching the recent life of her magnificent and unusual Son that God was about to do something spectacular through him.

The feast was delicious, and the singing and dancing were in full swing when Mary noticed they had run out of wine. Mary had always been good at noticing details. She stood next to Jesus, and in a low voice, she pointed out the problem. She knew how embarrassing that would be for her friends.

"Dear woman, why do you involve me?" Jesus replied. "My time has not yet come." Mary understood what he was telling her—he wanted to keep his identity secret for a while yet. Mary trusted his sense of timing but nodded to the servants who were nearby and told them quietly, "Do whatever he tells you" (John 2:4–5 NIV).

Nearby were six stone water jars, the kind the Jews used for ceremonial washing, and each held from twenty to thirty gallons. The servants hovered nervously near them, waiting for Jesus to speak or do something. Finally he said to the servants, "Fill the jars with water." The servants did what he said, and then Jesus told them, "Now draw some out and take it to the master of the banquet" (John 2:7–8 NIV).

Mary stood back and watched the unfolding drama with delight. The master of the banquet sampled the water that had been turned into wine, and his face lit up. He didn't know where it came from, but he called the bridegroom aside and told him, "Everyone brings out the choice wine first and then the cheaper wine after the guests have had too much to drink; but you have saved the best till now" (John 2:10 NIV).

What We Can Learn from Jesus' First Miracle at a Wedding in Cana

It's Natural to Run Out Occasionally

Catch us the foxes, the little foxes that spoil the vines, for our vines have tender grapes. My beloved is mine, and I am his.

Song of Solomon 2:15–16

When you have guests, there's nothing worse than running out of food or drink—but sometimes that happens. And we don't like to run out of our passion, but sometimes we do. We get tired. We are imperfect humans. Marriage can take a beating at the crossroads.

Each stage of marriage has potential to drain our passion for each other. When we are first married, while it's exciting and new, there is much to learn and many adjustments to make. Sometimes very difficult ones. Having babies and small children can leave us exhausted and sleep deprived. And having teenagers and maybe a two-career household can make life seem crazy, and we can lose each other in the whirl of it all.

But I especially believe that marriage is vulnerable at midlife. We may still be raising children, plus caring for elderly parents, plus making a living. There are financial pressures as well as physical problems. At menopause, our libido can disappear off the radar screen. The saying, "The spirit is willing but the flesh is weak" takes on new connotations! ("Honey, I love you to pieces, but I'm so tired . . .") We can face the stress of schedule adjustments (maybe spending more time together because of retirement) or of a changing focus because children are leaving home. It takes a while to understand how to be together, to learn how to enjoy one another rather than take out personal frustrations on each other. In midlife, losses happen, as

130

this is a time in life when many of us lose our parents and members of our extended family. At any crossroads, we are in a point of transition. This demands that some things change, some are lost, and some are gained.

It's also a time of life when we are busily involved in many things, and there's a danger of a growing separateness in our lives. After the children are gone, or we've given up our eighty-hour-a-week job, we can look at each other and ask, "Who are you? What do we have in common?" That's a strong signal that it's time to replenish the relationship! Even little things can drain the joy, the wonder, and the spontaneity from the relationship. No matter how long you have been married, it's possible to run out of passion. But when we invite Jesus to the wedding and then do what he says, our love can be renewed—even better than at first.

We Must Do What He Says

Mary told the servants, "Do what he tells you." Marriage truly can be better than ever if we do what Jesus says. Lots of times we can complicate how we want to get our needs met. We might become very analytical, sit around a lot, and wait for feelings. The good news is, we don't need to wait for the feelings of being in love—we can "do" love. What does it mean to do what he says? I believe it means that we love one another. We are kind to one another. We will lay down our lives for each other (I think that means truly listening to one another)! We speak the truth in love to each other. We treat one another as we want to be treated. These are not dramatic, new ideas. But when we love one another, love never fails. It bears fruit. The amazing thing about obeying Jesus is that feelings follow action. Blessings follow obedience.

You may need to renegotiate your marriage at this Selah place, learn to relate to each other in a fresh way, begin to treat one another in an intentional way, as Jesus would have you do. If possible, take a weekend trip somewhere, or even a day trip. A couple we know just took two weeks to camp together at Yosemite, since it was a place they'd never been before. In their early fifties, they still feel young. They have a lot to offer and intend to invest their lives in others, but they needed time to dream and plan. They said it was the best trip of their lives: They hiked every day and reconnected as they planned for the next phase of their marriage. Through many of the marriage retreats Bill and I lead, we see couples of all ages find renewed love—just by getting away and remembering why they first fell in love with each other.

Remember the Obvious, Celebrate the Ordinary

Jesus used a commodity that is so common and available—water! Lots of times we look for some earth-shaking way to renew our marriages. It is true that we may need to solve some long-standing anger issues or deal with some forgiveness and acceptance. But often marriages are restored through simple, kind things:

Prepare a favorite meal. Stop to consider what would make your spouse happy, then do it. Take time simply to focus on each other and enjoy each other for who and what you are in the common, ordinary day. Eat breakfast together. Do something fun together on Saturday.

Take time to make love. Sometimes the deep dialogues that we need to have about important issues are not as tense after we make love. Sometimes we just need to have some fun together and let an argument go. Karen said her marriage was energized when she realized she was arguing with her husband about the same things over and over. "There's a time just to realize with a little humor that I'm never going to change his point of view and to enjoy him as he is." Being right sometimes means agreeing to disagree, and leaving it at that.

Remember, too, that he may be going through some life-changing struggles and evaluations. Your crossroads moment is often a transition time, or Selah, for him as well. Two Selahs happening at once can create added stress. It's a good time to schedule trips away together, to try to reunite emotionally and relish one another again.

Appreciate your body. This is something very obvious and ordinary, yet so important to restoring our love. Dave and Claudia Arp write,

> Investments in your health are investments in your friendship with your spouse. . . . How long has it been since you've had a physical? When have you taken a hard look at your diet? Are you getting the exercise you need? If you want to enjoy the second half of life, take our advice: Take care of yourself; if you don't, no one else will![1]

This year Bill and I have made a fresh commitment to diet and exercise, and we can't begin to tell you how much better we feel, and how much better our relationship is as a consequence.

Fall in Love Again

Grow old along with me. The best is yet to be.

Robert Browning

Saving the best till last! Can it really be true? We are led to believe that the best is in our youth and that things go downhill from there. But Jesus has a way of turning things upside down. This wonderful story of Jesus turning water into wine speaks to me about how much we in this Selah time of life need to fall in love again.

Before you dismiss this chapter as only for those who are married, think again! Sometimes at a crossroads or in midlife, we fall out of love with life. We lose our sense of wonder. We get tired, a little jaded. But in this Selah time, Jesus can do a miracle to restore the joy, to help us see life with new eyes.

Rekindling Our Love in Marriage Is like Rekindling Our Love for Jesus

How like a love between a husband and wife is the love we have with Jesus—the perfect lover of our souls. Jesus commended the church at Ephesus for their good works, their faithfulness. But he said, "Nevertheless, this I have against you, that you have left your first love" (Rev. 2:4).

Sometimes following Jesus gets tedious. We lose the passion as we go through the motions: attend church, do good works, read the Bible, tithe. Sure, we're good, we're faithful. But the fire—the joy, the sense of discovery and wonder—is gone. The routine is boring, ho-hum. The cares of the world, disillusionment with other believers, fragments of unforgiveness, disobedience left unrecognized and unattended can add layer upon layer of distance.

In the end, it's distance that kills a relationship, kills the passion. And when too much distance separates you from your love, you are left with a sense of independence, of doggedly doing your own thing, because it's too costly or painful to deal with old business, to confront the real issues. Solomon called to his beloved, "Rise up! . . . O my dove, in the clefts of the rock, in the secret places, . . . let me see your countenance, let me hear your voice" (Song of Sol. 2:13–14). Jesus calls to us too: "Come to Me. . . . Take My yoke upon you and learn from Me" (Matt. 11:28–29).

When we find ourselves in a dry and stale place, the passion gone, with only a sense of going through the motions, it can be a wake-up call to pay attention to what's most important, and we need time alone with him—a Selah. A time to clear the slate and listen. A quiet time in the Word to open our hearts to ask, "Lord, how is my love for you? Am I doing my own thing? Or is your will a priority in my life?" During a Selah time with him, we can restate, "Lord, I am available to you. Keep my heart fresh and tender toward you. Never let my love for you be business as usual!"

Why is falling in love again part of women making a difference, of embracing their Second Callings? People who are filled with joy and wonder are contagious, influential.

Just when we think we are finished, there's no more joy, and life has turned into a dull, boring existence, Jesus reminds us that when we tell him we have run out of wine and offer him our ordinary lives, he can do something miraculous with them.

Let Your Marriage Survive the Seasons

When I was eighteen and married Bill, who was twenty-three, I thought I had married a guy who was going to be a pastor (at least that's what he told me). I fully expected that we would stay in the same community for thirty years, as my parents had done before me: live in the same house, attend the same church.

Bill thought he had married a starry-eyed blonde who would spend her entire energy on homemaking (like his mother, who was the grand champion apple pie baker of Santa Cruz County)! It didn't quite work out like that. I didn't know I'd married a risk taker who loved nothing more than developing things, and Bill didn't know he'd married an independent, analytical woman driven to write. When I met Bill, I was quite impressed with his take-charge ways. He was charmed by my spontaneity and easygoing nature. Five years later, his take-charge ways felt in some ways controlling and domineering, and my spontaneity and easygoing nature seemed to Bill sometimes like failure to confront and a lack of boundaries.

Wow! That's why we need Jesus to come to our marriages. We can have very unrealistic expectations of each other, and the stressors of life influence our marriage relationships—and all our other relationships too, for that matter. In our marriages, we go through seasons: the newlywed years; the years of gathering and building careers and homes; the sending-off years, when we send our kids to college, into marriage; what Bill and I have discovered as the wonderful years of grandparenting; and finally senior-citizen years.

We sink or swim through these changing seasons. At the crossroads, a woman can be surprised to learn how strong she is, and her husband may be threatened by her newfound confidence. This is a vulnerable time in a marriage, and sometimes, instead of working through the rough places, a woman can be tempted to see her husband as excess baggage and divorce him. A woman told me with a wicked grin, "Do you know why husbands are like bras in midlife? You'd like to strip them off and go free, but you need the support!"

Well, I have to say, I not only need the support, I want it! In many circles, divorce is almost a rite of passage for a woman on the move. Divorce happens, but even when there are good reasons for it, the pain and long-term consequences are deep and real. While our thirty-six-year marriage, like all unions, has been a work in progress, Bill and I are more in love with each other than ever before. Marriage is something of a mystery: Two very different people from very different backgrounds (not to mention gender differences!) join together to create a family, a home, and a legacy. It is a precious and powerful thing. Your marriage is worth saving!

Bill and I lead a lot of marriage retreats that keep us motivated to work on our own relationship. We were telling our son about some of the sessions we were teaching, one of them on sex, and Chris said, "I just can't go there! I prefer to think of my parents as really, really good friends." We laughed and told him we were good friends—but thank God, we were also more than friends! The sexual relationship is a wonderful gift that keeps a couple lovers, as well as friends, throughout life. And it is true that in many surveys, the number-one quality that couples cherish in their relationship is their friendship.

Your marriage doesn't have to be a statistic. Couples aren't supposed to be in love forever—even when life drains them dry. Well, with God all things are possible.

Bill and I are learning to move from a child-centered relationship to a couple-centered one. This is quite a process, especially because we have five children, one of whom has special needs, and grandbabies have come into the family. It does not mean that children are any less our priority, or our hearts. We still love them with everything we have, and we still pray daily; we still have influence, but the dynamic has changed. We are moving into a new place.

One day I tried to find Bill to tell him about some exciting new idea I had, and I found him in his workshop—making birdhouses! I was astounded. He looked up, grinning and covered with sawdust. Now, these are not ordinary birdhouses. They are log houses with Adirondack chairs in front, and he's donating them to our local school for a fund-raiser. But as a driven woman who is not known for hobbies, I can't relate to making birdhouses.

I think Bill was saying, "Hey, I've already tried to change the world, and while I'm still working, I'm enjoying puttering in my workshop!" He's finding pleasure in the Selah time of life, and I'm ready to do that with him—just not in his workshop! We're learning to savor just being together. We have some favorite places to look at wildflowers and find interesting rocks for our pathway. We just bought new bikes and like to go riding.

Often a man at this stage of life is ready to relax, not be so intense. He wants companionship, and if his wife is off on her agenda, the marriage may suffer. In his loneliness, he may end up looking for a "buddy" elsewhere.

If you are not yet in that place in your marriage, and you think it's way off in the future, think again. It comes sooner than you think, and it's time now to cultivate your relationship, no matter where you are in your marriage. We all want to have the glow of love forever. But, as I can tell from experience, it doesn't just happen. It is an ongoing process, a constant challenge as life ebbs and flows, the stresses and circumstances changing.

And we find in our marriages that the process of staying in love must be constantly reevaluated. Protected. Redefined.

There is a unique element between a man and a woman that is like a spark of electricity, a fire, a twinkle. Thousands of songs and poems have been written about its power, charm, and loss, attempting to capture its mystery by invoking images of the stars, the heavens, the wind, and a thousand other metaphors. It is called passionate romance. None of us really understand romance or sexual passion, yet we as humans are nearly all drawn to it and its powerful emotions. It is as old as human beings can remember.

I love the fact that stuck smack-dab in the middle of God's holy Word is a "Song of Songs" written by one of the wisest men in history to his lover. He calls it a song "more wonderful than any other." And yet this wisest of men is obviously consumed by the magnetic chemistry of this love. Read it and you see hot passion on every page. What will tend to dampen passion? Many things, but here are a few of the more common ones many couples have shared with us: men who want sex without paying the price of good communication; women who nag; spouses who take each other for granted; the failure to keep "courting" each other; ongoing, never-resolved arguments; poor hygiene; and stress of all kinds (money, in-laws, overcrowded schedules, etc.).

What keeps the passion fires burning? The opposite of the things listed above that dampen romance, of course. Add to these things attitudes of tenderness; loving surprises (flowers, unexpected notes, little gifts); time spent together in mutually enjoyable activities.

> My darling bride is like a private garden, a spring that no one else can have, a fountain of my own.
>
> Song of Solomon 4:12 TLB

Take Responsibility for Yourself as a Wife

In this pause of life, in the sometimes-quiet moments, we may find some leftover expectations, unresolved anger, or long-held resentments. What do we do with them? One of the most important things I have learned in my marriage is to stop blaming. I didn't realize how subtly blame was eroding my marriage.

Since I married so young and started having babies when I was just twenty-one, my dream of finishing college was unrealized. I worked to help Bill through his master's program, and I never actually told him so, but I blamed him for my not continuing my education. Playing blame games, even when we don't verbalize them, can seep into a relationship and cause deep damage. My inward thought was *I never realized my dream, and it's all your fault!*

To be fair to Bill, he did not know it was that important to me. I had given him every indication that marrying him, having a family, and following his calling in ministry was my purpose. And it was—but at eighteen years of age, I did not really know my own mind. I think I was operating largely out of raging hormones and need!

We can be very threatened by differences. Different does not necessarily mean defective; it means *different*. Gretchen and Eric have been married eight years and have two small children. They married early and still had some growing up to do. They told us, "Our most difficult struggle is to accept one another as we are. We wanted so much from one another and were constantly disappointed." A turning point came at a retreat when Gretchen was challenged to specifically thank God for what he had given her. She began to thank God for Eric—even if he wasn't living up to her expectations. She began to look at him with different eyes, and he found it easier to change.

It can be tempting to look to our mates to fill up all our emotional needs and fall into a parenting role with one another. This is not a healthy pattern for a long-term marriage. You can't validate your spouse when you are in a parenting mode—God has not created you as the parent of your spouse; he has created you as the *partner* of your spouse. Acceptance that each of us has certain needs is an important step toward a long-lasting love relationship. We can help one another with our needs when we recognize that we do each have our needs and that we cannot change one another but we can try to understand and accept one another.

A marriage must grow past blaming. If you haven't already done so, now is the perfect time to take responsibility for yourself, your own stuff. As long as we blame our husbands, or blame our bosses, or blame the president, we haven't really taken responsibility for ourselves. Maybe you've even blamed God! But blaming keeps us from growing into the women we can be.

Marriage isn't for children, and vows are kept by adults.

Focus on Each Other Again

Work on Your Friendship

In survey after survey, at least 80 percent of couples in successful long-term relationships report that they have

become best friends. . . . They feel accepted with their faults
and have come to accept their mates as a package deal.

Dr. Georgia Witkin, How to Keep Intimacy Alive

Lois Jean Davitz surveyed four hundred divorced men
between the ages of twenty and forty-five and revealed
some surprising contradictions to popular myths about
why marriages fail.

"What virtually every man in our study cited as decisive
to the failure of the relationship was the lack of companionship," she said. And how did these men define companionship? Doing enjoyable things with their spouses, spending
recreational time together. Davitz saw a man's desire for
female companionship as a shift in expectations. "In the
past," she said, "men often turned to other men for companionship, but today, they'd rather spend time with their
wives." Unfortunately, this shift comes at a time when many
women are feeling overwhelmed by their multiple roles as
wage earners, home managers, wives, and mothers. Wrote
Davitz, "As women struggle to meet expanded challenges,
there's a very real danger that the men they love are being
squeezed out of their lives."[2]

Keep Hope Alive

O my dove, in the clefts of the rock, in the secret places of
the cliff, let me see your face, let me hear your voice; for
your voice is sweet, and your face is lovely.

Song of Solomon 2:14

Love sees the best. When we first marry, most of us have a
strong sense of optimism about the future. It doesn't take
long to discover that we've married an imperfect human
being, with his own set of flaws. Our expectations can be

dashed if we begin to focus on the negative aspects of our spouses.

Optimistic love can carry us a long way through the circumstances of life. When your spouse suffers a setback, you can help by focusing on the bright side. Or you can further entrench your husband's depression or fear by being negative. Words are powerful. I'm not suggesting that you ignore the problem or deny that it exists. This can be equally damaging. But remind each other that there is always hope!

When we focus on hope rather than despair, we help one another to see the joy in life. We are vulnerable to each other's words and can influence our spouses as no one else can. Henri Amiel wrote these profound words: "Sweet thoughts, kind whispers, a listening ear, and a helping hand—these are the things that speak your beloved's language. No special setting can take the place of word and deed given from the heart. Life is short and we never have too much time for gladdening the hearts of those who travel the way with us. Oh, be swift to love! Make haste to be kind."[3]

Take Time to Play

Being playful is the cotton candy of any meat-and-potatoes relationship. It's the . . . let's-have-a-party, let's-skip-work-and-go-to-the-beach, let's-rent-three-videos-and-watch-them-all-tonight state of mind that lifts a relationship from the tedious and banal to the extraordinary and effervescent. We forget to play, or we never learned how. We are worked so hard and so long by life as it is—and by our own ambitions—that most of us don't play nearly enough.

Daphne Rose Kingma, *Garland of Love*

Medical science is now beginning to discover what a very wise man knew several thousand years ago. King

Solomon said, "A merry heart does good, like medicine" (Prov. 17:22). Humor can be a powerful tool in marriage building.

In her article "Go Ahead . . . Laugh," Nancy Kennedy reports on a study done by William Fry, a psychiatrist, laugh researcher, and professor emeritus at Stanford University Medical School (how would you like his job?). Fry says that deep belly laughs benefit the entire body because the whole physiology of the person laughing is involved. A hearty laugh gives the heart a cardiovascular workout and massages the muscles in the face, diaphragm, and abdomen. The psychiatrist says that laughing also lowers blood pressure. Evidently, it is indeed good medicine to laugh.[4]

It's possible to miss real life while slogging through the one you have. Too often we put off taking time simply to see the wonder around us, as we get so involved with our routines. We plod on, thinking someday we will feel better, laugh more, enjoy each other. Take time to celebrate along the way.

Honor Your Marriage with Selah

> The point of marriage is not to create a quick commonality by tearing down all boundaries; on the contrary, a good marriage is one in which each partner appoints the other to be the guardian of his solitude, and thus they show each other the greatest possible trust.
>
> Robert Hass and Stephen Mitchell, *Into the Garden:*
> *A Wedding Anthology*[5]

When we married, Bill gave me a beautiful little pendant on a gold chain. It is two leaves with a pearl in the middle. To me, the pearl between those two gold leaves symbolizes the holy ground between us—the God-shaped vacuum that only he can fill. In our mobile, transient society, we can

143

be tempted to expect our spouses to meet all our needs. A truly passionate relationship needs Selah—some times to be quietly alone while we are together. Or as a poet described it, "space in our togetherness." Each of us brings something unique and precious to our marriage relation-ship, and if we do not respect our spouse's uniqueness, we tend to desecrate our potential for intimacy.

Think of it this way. In order to play musical harmony, it takes two parts. If you are both singing the same note, you may have unanimity but not harmony. Harmony is much sweeter music and more interesting than a one-note monotone. The same is true in marriage. Respect for the part the other plays in the marriage is far more beautiful and pleasing than insisting he or she act and sound just like you. It's helpful when we learn to appreciate our spouse's uniqueness.

Intimacy is holy ground. When your spouse lets you inside the deepest parts of his heart, be careful to tread softly and recognize that you are in a sacred place. Within the context of a committed marriage, life with its demands can at times drain passion from a marriage. But love can be renewed, refreshed, and restored when we revisit our first love.

This principle seems to have a biblical precedent. In Revelation Jesus says to the church in Ephesus, "Yet there is one thing wrong; you don't love me as at first! Think about those times of your first love (how different now!) and turn back to me again and work as you did before" (Rev. 2:4–5 TLB).

Remember how you acted when you first fell in love? Do the same things; treat each other again the way you did when you first were in love and watch the results. Brenda, married five years and with two small children told us, "We got so busy raising kids, working, taking care of our house that we literally forgot to connect in every way—physically, emotionally, and spiritually. It's amazing what happened when we went away just the two of us for a few days recently and were absolutely lost in each other again. It's wonderful!"

But it's possible to connect in the ordinary days too. My mother used to tell me after the too-early death of my father, "Don't wait for someday to enjoy each other. Learn to savor every day." We have this precious moment—that is all! So often we are rushing ahead, rushing to work, rushing to make deadlines. It doesn't take that much to renew love; it's just stopping to see someone you love—really see him. To see the beauty that is all around us, if we will just look: the magnificent sky, a beautiful flower. To savor the fact that God made us, he loves us, and he will restore us if we simply ask.

Prayer

Lord, you have given us to each other, and yet there are many things in our world that would drain the joy from life. Help us remember when our love was new and our passion was high. We pray for obedient and willing hearts in order to do your will—to love one another as you love us. Thank you for showing us that the closer we become to you, the closer we become to one another. Rekindle the flame in us. Amen.

Mapping Your Next Step

Read the story of Jesus turning the water into wine in John 2; also read the Song of Solomon.

- What insights for your own life does the story of Jesus turning the water into wine give you?

- Think of some concrete ways you can invite Jesus in to help you celebrate life.
- If you are married, what qualities first attracted you to your spouse?
- In what three ways can you strengthen your friendship with your spouse?
- What words or statements tend to shut down communication in your marriage?
- What words or statements help advance God's presence in your marriage?
- Read one or all of these helpful books with a friend and discuss:

    The Gift of Sex by Cliff and Joyce Penner

    The Second Half of Marriage by Dave and Claudia Arp

    The Five Love Languages by Gary Chapman

    Lord Bless This Marriage by William and Nancie Carmichael

PART 3

Your Second Calling

This has the potential to be the most fulfilling time of our lives. It is when we let go of the nonessentials in order to follow our new calling—which is often a ripening or deepening of our First Calling.

If we are making a quilt, this is a most creative time of putting the pieces together to make the beautiful design. It may be time for some bold moves. Some pieces need to be discarded, as you used many of them in another quilt, or they are not the right fabric and wouldn't fit the piece you're working on now. You want good quality material that will last. After all, it's unique—one of a kind! And it is a legacy you will be pleased to pass on to others. It's not just pretty; it's for something. It's useful.

In answering the Second Calling, we're ready to engage in something substantial. It is a time to risk taking steps of faith. It is a time to be deeply hungry to learn, to grow, to give, to spend our lives wisely. What a wonderful place to be in life—a time to give away ourselves . . . and in the giving, receive in knowing we are making a difference.

147

9

Letting Go

Naomi:
Divesting

When one door of happiness closes, another opens;
but often we look so long at the closed door that we
do not see the one which has been opened for us.

Helen Keller

Naomi was a charming woman who held an unshakable belief that the best was just around the corner. And then it seemed that every corner she turned, the best was a mirage that kept moving farther away from her. She and her husband, Elimelech, and two sons, Mahlon and Kilion, lived in Bethlehem, but due to a famine in the land, they moved to Moab, as they'd heard there was more opportunity there.

A few years after their move, Elimelech died. Naomi was devastated, but she had to keep going for the sake of her sons. She went on a diligent search to find good wives for them and was pleased to discover Ruth and Orpah, local women. And then it seemed that the unraveling of her life accelerated, as first one of her sons grew very ill and died; then the other son, within a short time, also died. Naomi felt that her whole life consisted of funerals and burials and grieving. She was inconsolable. How could she go on? Her husband and sons were her world, and now her world was gone—except for her daughters-in-law, whom she had grown to love. In a foreign land, with two foreign daughters-in-law, Naomi was torn about what to do.

She heard the famine was over in Bethlehem, and something inside her urged, *Go home.* Perhaps there she could live among her people and get some comfort, remembering the happy years when Elimelech was alive, and Mahlon and Kilion were small, and their hopes were high.

One morning, as she and Orpah and Ruth worked together to put their husbands' belongings away, they wept over their heartrending task. Naomi stopped, suddenly seeing her two daughters-in-law. They were so young. She told them, "Go back, each of you, to your mother's home. May the LORD show kindness to you, as you have shown to your dead and to me. May the LORD grant that each of you will find rest in the home of another husband" (Ruth 1:8–9 NIV). Naomi hugged and kissed them, her eyes filled with tears again as she remembered the joyful weddings, the dreams her own sons had had for children. Now those dreams were gone.

Orpah kissed Naomi good-bye and left. But Ruth was another matter. "Don't urge me to leave you or to turn back from you. Where you go I will go, and where you stay I will stay. Your people will be my people and your God my God," she told Naomi (Ruth 1:16 NIV).

It was a long and dusty journey, and when the two women arrived in Bethlehem, people were excited to see them. "Naomi, is it really you?" Naomi gave a short laugh of derision. She knew her name meant "pleasant." Her life lately had been anything but that. "Don't call me Naomi," she said curtly. "Call me Mara, because the Almighty has made my life very bitter. I went away full, but the LORD has brought me back empty" (Ruth 1:20–21 NIV). It seemed that God was out to get her.

But the necessity of staying alive—and Ruth—helped fill the days. Boaz, one of Naomi's relatives from Elimelech's side of the family, was a wealthy man with large fields. It was the custom that after the harvesters went through the fields, poor people were allowed to gather the grain that was left. While Ruth was out gathering grain in Boaz's field, he noticed her, and his foreman told him who she was.

Boaz had heard of this remarkable young woman and told her, "Don't go and glean in another field. . . . Stay here with my servant girls. . . . I've been told all about what you have done for your mother-in-law since the death of your husband—how you left your father and mother and your homeland and came to live with a people you did not know before. . . . May you be richly rewarded by the LORD, the God of Israel, under whose wings you have come to take refuge" (Ruth 2:8, 11–12 NIV).

During a break in the harvest, Boaz invited her to share a meal of roasted grain, and she even had some left over for Naomi. Boaz gave orders to his men to leave extra grain for her, which they did. That evening, she returned home with nearly a bushel! Naomi was glad to hear of Boaz's kindness, and a plan began hatching in her mind. She told Ruth, "That man is our close relative; he is one of our kinsman-redeemers" (Ruth 2:20 NIV).

A kinsman-redeemer was a close, influential relative to whom members of the extended family could turn for help, usually when the family line was in danger of being lost. He was supposed to buy back family land sold during a crisis, provide an heir for a dead brother, or care for relatives in difficult circumstances. Naomi saw new possibilities and instructed Ruth to dress in her best, wash and anoint herself with perfume, and go where Boaz was working on the threshing floor. Naomi told her not to let him see her until after he'd eaten and was lying down to sleep. She instructed, "Note the place where he is lying. Then go and uncover his feet and lie down. He will tell you what to do" (Ruth 3:4 NIV).

When Ruth got home the next morning, she told Naomi about the amazing evening: how, in the middle of the night, Boaz was startled and woke up, and Ruth told him, "Spread the corner of your garment over me, since you are a kinsman-redeemer" (Ruth 3:9 NIV).

As events unfolded, Boaz took Ruth to be his wife. In time, Ruth gave birth to a son, and Naomi's arms were full once more. Naomi gazed with wonder and joy at the precious baby sleeping in her arms and agreed with what the local women had told her: "He will renew your life and sustain you in your old age. For your daughter-in-law, who loves you and who is better to you than seven sons, has given him birth" (Ruth 4:15 NIV).

The years of letting go of her dearest hopes and dreams had been difficult. But God renewed and sustained Naomi with new life that she never dreamed possible.

What Can We Learn from Naomi?

When Naomi started her life with Elimelech, she didn't plan on all the losses she would suffer. So it is with us. The First Calling of our lives is a time of gathering in—of working, perhaps marrying and having children, buying homes and filling them with stuff. Most of us don't really think about the letting-go business until later—in the Second Calling of our lives—and then life gives us wake-up calls.

In midlife or at certain crossroads, we are called to let go of a lot, and the most difficult is our children. Many of us are losing our parents too, or we realize as we watch our peers lose theirs that we won't have ours forever. My friend Carol, a schoolteacher, echoed what many of us feel; she said that losing her mother was a pivotal loss in her life, even though it gave her peace to know that her mother was in God's presence. C. S. Lewis wrote about the passing of his own mother: "With my mother's death, all settled happiness, all that was tranquil and reliable, disappeared from my life. There was to be much fun, many pleasures, many stabs of joy; but no more of the old security. It was sea and islands now; the great continent has sunk like Atlantis."[1]

Grieve the Losses You Experience

Naomi and her daughters-in-law wept openly about their losses. Some of the things we must let go of—a family member, a parent, a spouse—are obviously deep losses that we must grieve. It's important to be honest about these, to give them their space. But there are other things in our lives that we are called to let go of that are more subtle. You may be feeling the loss of your identity as wife, due to death or divorce. In a divorce, you can also lose certain extended family members who meant more to you than you'd realized. Or there may be the loss of your title in the change of a work situation or responsibility.

There is also the very real letting go of thinking of one-self as young, or as one of the movers and shakers. One woman wrote,

> As I grow older, I often find myself in the invisible genera-
> tion. This means I may have to be willing to make a differ-
> ence unheralded and unseen. Nothing wrong with that, but
> for some who are not prepared, it may seem discouraging
> or even crushing. But I've found that many crucial things
> women can do in their second half of life—such as the
> ultra-important task of intercessory prayer—are done in a
> closet, alone. Helping others in need, volunteering, or being
> a caregiver are pretty much done without a lot of fanfare.

The day I took my son Andy to kindergarten, I saw a friend sobbing outside the school. She'd just brought her only son to kindergarten. "My life is over," she wailed. I tried to assure her that her life was definitely not over. But it is true that when children leave home (and thankfully, they leave in stages), one of the most important jobs we'll ever have is over: the day-to-day concern and care of our most precious gift, our children.

Now that I look back, I see that it was easy to lose myself in nurturing a family as well as in building a business with my husband. Without a doubt, motherhood has been the most difficult, most challenging yet rewarding calling of my life. And as is true with all great causes, in losing myself in it, I found myself. It is such a defining role. Although we never stop loving our kids, letting go of that calling as we knew it is difficult.

Letting go is a process that takes time. After we sold our much-loved family home, we built a new one, which we love too. So we still have *home*, with all the familiar pictures and furniture; we just don't have children there all the time. The family still comes home for holidays and special occasions, especially Thanksgiving and Christmas and Easter.

Easter has always been a very special time for our family. On the Saturday night before Easter morning, I hid prizes all over the house with notes for clues, and we woke in the morning to the sound of bare feet running all over, up and down the stairs. The hunt for prizes and eggs would end at a sign saying: "Hallelujah, he is risen!"

Usually, all or most of our children get home for Easter—until this year, that is. It started falling apart on the Thursday before Easter. Jon and Brittni and their three children couldn't make it due to Jon's work schedule. Chris and Jami needed to be in Portland with her family. Andy had to be in Portland to meet his girlfriend's plane. One by one, our plans fell through. I spent most of Saturday going to Target and Wal-Mart, returning surprises I had bought.

Sunday morning I got up early, made coffee, and went upstairs to the loft to read my Bible. I read about the women coming to the empty tomb, with the angel asking them, "Why do you seek the living among the dead?" (Luke 24:5).

All day that question came to me: *Why seek the living among the dead? Is that what I have been doing? Trying to extract purpose from something that is finished?* The empty nest now was not just a cliché or a phrase; it was real. The emptiness was palpable. The afternoon before, I'd gone on a walk, thinking, *Why did I even buy that Easter lily? What is the point? At least I won't have to work so hard. Bill and I will go to church and sing four verses of "He Arose" and rejoice, that's what we'll do!* All these things I was saying to myself as I tromped on the trail behind our house, going along a creek shaded by trees.

When I finally let myself be still, it seemed God was saying, "I am helping you to let go. Don't resist it." I thought I had been handling that season of life pretty well. I was actually enjoying it. But my empty Easter reminded me what a huge transition this really is in my life. Motherhood can be so consuming, and we have such a big family that one of the kids is usually around, so it's possible to operate under the illusion that mothering is still my primary purpose—but this last Easter I had a sharp reminder that life was changing.

"It's time," Bill sagely reminded me, "to realize the kids have grown up." We ended up having a wonderful church service and then brunch with Eric, Carly, Amy, and another couple. But I have to admit there was a huge lump in my throat that I couldn't swallow for two days. No children in my house on Easter morning!

Not long after this, a young mother said to me, "I would love to establish some of our own traditions, but my mother-in-law wants to do it all the time. I don't want to hurt her feelings, but how do I let her know we'd like to do our own thing sometimes?" I winced inside with fresh wisdom and told her, "You are exactly right to establish your own traditions. Tell her gently but firmly what your plans are. Chances are, she will be glad for the rest. Ask for a recipe, or include her in your own celebration, if possible. There may be times you want to crash at her house and enjoy a holiday."

Children leave in an ever-widening circle, moving away from needing hands-on parenting. While I know with my head that a good mother works herself out of a job, it still hurts. Martin Luther, who suffered many losses in his life, said these words of wisdom: "I have held many things in my hand, and have lost them all. But that which I have placed in God's hands, that I still possess."

Make New Plans

Naomi's healing began when she took the first step to go back to Bethlehem. As she got caught up in the rhythms of life—becoming a matchmaker for Ruth—her healing continued.

My sister Judy, who had to make a new life after a divorce, said she took intentional steps in her new community that helped her recover. She planted something permanent, a rosebush, because it meant she would have something to nourish in that new place. She subscribed to the local paper and got a library card, as well as an Oregon driver's license. She joined a church and became an active participant. These deliberate actions helped her let go of her old identity in order to rebuild a new one.

After my Easter fiasco, Bill and I talked it over and realized we had entered a new phase. While we want our children to know that we love it when they can come home, if they can't, we will be fine! There may be holidays when we will do things together, or we'll be with friends when our children cannot be here. It's not a time to feel sorry for ourselves or to make our children feel guilty. We can help them develop their own lives by freeing them to develop their own families and traditions.

My mother's example encourages me. Her life was full with seven children, with leadership in our church, with our 4-H club, and with helping my father, so she had little time for personal pursuits. Letting go of all of us was not easy for her. I knew, however, that she always longed to write, and as some of us began leaving home, she took a writer's course by mail and eventually succeeded in selling a few of her short stories. After we all left home, she and my father relocated to Oregon. When my father died, she was really alone. She could have felt sorry for herself, but after some grieving, like Naomi she got involved in others' lives and began teaching women's Bible studies. She developed a fanatical interest in basketball; in fact, she named her canary Larry Bird. Her great delight was her children and grandchildren, her neighbors, and anybody who happened into her life.

I gratefully and joyfully accept the times I have with my children and grandchildren—but they are bonus moments. Mothering is not the centerpiece of my life now. I see that I cannot depend on my children to justify my existence for the rest of my life (or the rest of theirs). We are powerful influencers to them, always—with a word or two, a look, an expression, we can generate a lot of guilt. You may have seen the bumper sticker "My mother is a West Coast guilt distributor."

The story is told of a telephone conversation between a mother who knew how to dish out guilt and her grown son:

Son: Mom, hi. How are you? How's everything in Florida?
Mom: Not too good. I've been very weak.
Son: Why are you weak?
Mom: Never mind.

Son: Why are you weak, Mom?
Mom: I haven't eaten in thirty-eight days.
Son: That's terrible. Why haven't you eaten in thirty-eight days?
Mom: Because I didn't want my mouth to be filled with food if you should call.[2]

Invest in Others

Ruth and Boaz named their child Obed—meaning "service." Naomi found fulfillment in letting go of her grief and bitterness to become involved in Ruth's life. She offered Ruth her services, counseling her, and then later caring for baby Obed. Fulfillment and healing come when we invest in others. There are countless ways we can continue our nurturing; we just need to look around us. Many of the elderly in rest homes and in neighborhoods near us would love some company; we know people who are lonely and need to be listened to and reminded that they are important. This helps us shift our focus from ourselves to seeing the needs of those around us.

We can volunteer in our communities and make a huge difference in the lives of children and young people who need caring adults. We can teach a Sunday school class or take a turn in the church nursery. Many times when children leave home, we are tempted to think, *Been there, done that,* when we have so much to offer! We need to be aware of where we can offer our services and then do it.

I have come to see that I can offer my services to our children and grandchildren. Since Bill and I are still involved in speaking, writing, and traveling, I give them dates on the calendar when we are home and available. But I admit that if my children really need me, I do everything I can to be there.

Bill and I just spent three very fun days with Jon and Brittni and their three children. Bill helped Jon build a deck in their backyard, and I helped Brittni with six-year-old Willy's birthday party. When we let go of our old roles, we are free to have new ones. I may not be the ringmaster of the circus, but I can be a clown in the corner (which is a whole lot more fun)!

If you're not a grandparent yet, believe me: Every wonderful thing people say about it is true. As my friend Dorothy says, "It's God's reward to you for getting old!" It is a time in life when we move aside; we become servants. This is a new role. I hold babies, rock them, go to the store, change a diaper. I tell stories, read. I help three-year-old Kendsy ride her bike to the park. I see it as playing, really. (And then when we are worn-out, we hug and kiss them good-bye, and go home!)

Midlife is also a good time to reinvest in our relationships with our friends and siblings (not to mention spouses). They are touchstones through the years who keep reminding us of who we are. In a way, relationships with close friends and siblings do not change, and they do not require us to change. We have a history together, and the empty-nest time of life is a prime time to strengthen those relationships.

Let Go of Destructive Emotions

Naomi had to let go of her bitterness before her life was enjoyable again. Ask yourself, *What am I clinging to that I need to let go?* We can't live effective lives when we're loaded down with things of the past: bitterness, what-ifs, fears, regrets. The writer of Hebrews encourages us in chapter 12 to "lay aside every weight, and the sin which so easily ensnares us, and let us run with endurance the race that is set before us" (v. 1). The rest of the chapter reminds us to be careful not to stumble, to pursue wholeness and peace, to deal with root causes of bitterness, and most of all, to accept God's grace.

It's also a time to recognize regrets, deal with them, and come to terms with losses and disappointments. It's important to acknowledge them, to let them go and move on. It is a time to look at the blessings we have in our lives and be grateful.

We may even need to let go of a longing for the good old days, or how things used to be. We may have regrets, thinking, *If only I had done this instead of that . . .* Rage at injustice is difficult to let go. Sometimes we may feel, as Naomi did, that the hand of God is against us. Job wrote thousands of years ago, "I am desperate because God the all-powerful refuses to do what is right" (see 27:1–2). At times, the fury of injustice cuts deep, and we shout, "I gave you the best years of my life, and look how you treated me!" Or "I've done everything I can to parent you, love you. How can you behave this way? I taught you better!" Or we may be stuck believing: *I gave my best to this company—I was loyal, I went the second mile, and they terminated my whole department.*

A friend sent me this story: Two friends were walking through the desert. During some point of the journey they had an argument, and one friend slapped the other in the face. The one who got slapped was hurt, but without saying anything, he wrote in the sand: "Today my best friend slapped me in the face."

They kept on walking until they found an oasis, where they decided to take a swim. The one who had been slapped got a cramp and started drowning, but the friend saved him. After the friend recovered from the near drowning, he chiseled on a stone: "Today my best friend saved my life."

The friend who had slapped and saved his best friend asked him, "After I hurt you, you wrote in the sand, and now, you write on a stone. Why?"

His friend replied, "When someone hurts us, we should write it down in sand, where winds of forgiveness can erase it. But when someone does something good for us, we must engrave it in stone, where no wind can ever erase it."

Do not look forward to the changes and chances of this in fear; rather look to them with full hope that, as they arise, God, whose you are, will deliver you out of them. He is your keeper. He has kept you hitherto. Do you but hold fast to his dear hand, and he will lead you safely through all things; and, when you cannot stand, he will bear you in his arms. Do not look forward to what may happen tomorrow. Our Father will either shield you from suffering, or he will give you strength to bear it.[3]

Grab On to the New

As we take a clear-eyed look at where we are in life, we must be sure we are letting go in order to grab on to the good things: personal Bible study and honest, real relationships. We must be willing to empty out old expectations, regrets, and destructive emotions to make way for dreaming some new dreams. Revelation 3:2 says: "Be watchful, and strengthen the things which remain." What remains? What is worth keeping as we let go? First Corinthians 13 says, "These things remain: faith, hope and love. And the greatest of these is love" (see v. 13).

How good it is to think about the hopeful blessings, the promises we have in our lives, and to look on what we do have and not on what we don't. How good it is to show mercy and grace, to let some old scores and resentments go. When we refuse to let go of what we are gripping so tightly, we aren't free for the next step God has for us.

Let Change Come

As time passes, we let go of our family as we've known it. I see my siblings experience this too as our get-togethers with the cousins are changing. Now we stay in touch with the occasional wedding or graduation or funeral. We tell each other that we're doing good just to get our own kids together now.

I have mentioned that last year, we decided to let go of our family house, where Bill and I lived for twenty-three years with our children. During this process, one afternoon the phone rang. It was the realtor, wanting to show the house to a prospective client in half an hour. Andy, our youngest twenty-something son, had come home late from Portland, and when I went down the next morning to the kitchen, I found the For Sale sign that he'd pulled out of the ground in front of our house. He'd placed it on the dining room table with an emphatic note: "I do not like this.—Roo"

None of us liked it, but it was a wise financial steward-ship step that we needed to take. The day before, I'd taken apart the kids' old sandbox, raked the yard of needles, and spread the sand over the grass. In some ways, I felt as if I were scattering ashes: no more making sand castles under the canopy of the big pine tree.

Before I left, I walked through my house, wondering what those who were looking for a home would see there. It seemed to me to be a peace-filled house. I wiped the fingerprints off the door to the deck, put the ever-present basketball in the garage in the sports box. The carpets were freshly vacuumed, wood floors gleaming. The house smelled of vanilla and lemon, and strains of Beethoven played in the background. The welcome mat out front was swept and clean. The crimson ivy geraniums filled the deck off the back of the house, and hummingbirds hovered to get their sweet nectar. Good-bye, my house.

To depart is to die a little. But to stay is to die a little too. One must have a place before one can give it up. One must receive before giving, exist before abandoning oneself in faith. We receive a place only so as eventually to leave it, treasure only so as to cast it away, a personal existence only so as to be able to offer it up.[4]

It Hurts to Let Go

The world changes. And if your family is like ours, it's a gradual process. I wrote this piece the year I turned forty, when our children first began leaving home:

Home again—finally. We stumble through the doorway, weary from our two-day trip. Bill engineers the kids from the outside, giving them suitcases, sleeping bags and miscellaneous loads of whatever it is people take on trips. I direct them from the kitchen, intercepting dirty laundry before it disappears upstairs.

Three children left. We had gone to southern California to escort our two oldest sons to college since we had a van and could fill it with everything that wouldn't fit in their Honda—clothes, bedding, furnishings. It had helped the younger three that the college is near Disneyland. So we'd had fun too.

As we drove home toward Oregon, I had looked at our remaining three with new eyes. For some reason Chris, Andrew and Amy seemed larger now—more like real people. I had a flashback. I was at the hospital with a new baby, about to go home to the baby's older sibling, who suddenly was immense. Or so it seemed then.

Did my youngest three really fill up more space now, or had we been pouring that much energy into Jon and Eric? The final two years of childhood are much like the first two—a lot of molding and finessing go into a child just before he takes flight.

Now there's Chris—suddenly six feet tall at age 16 and wearing a size-12 shoe. My quiet, introspective son, now looking like a man. And Andrew—13 and still loving boyhood. And teasing his sister. However, some signs of things to come: Andy's voice is deepening. His prayers are thoughtful these days. He loves God, and life is immense to him, holy and sacred.

And then there's Amy—part my baby, part a wise woman from the East. Our 9-year-old adopted daughter—once

163

abandoned in Korea, now in the market for a training bra. Now we're home again, the house silently happy to see us—the remnant of its family. Bill is going through ten days' worth of mail, Chris already is fielding phone calls, and Amy's playing with Spooky the cat and exulting in having her own room.

I put the dirty clothes in the strangely clean laundry room. Funny. I hadn't seen the floor all summer. It is yellow, after all. No duffel bags, golf bags or basketball shoes. How nice. But of course—two fewer boys translates into less laundry. So why do I have this lump in my throat? Chris is calling from upstairs. "Mom, when can I move up?"

"Move? You mean to Jon and Eric's room?"

"Right!"

"Now, wait." I climb the stairs slowly, hesitating before the boys' room, afraid of ghosts. "I don't know that we're ready to do this. Can't it wait until tomorrow?"

He's already in there, irreverently trashing old posters, moving beds, emptying a dresser drawer of worn-out basketball jerseys and outgrown jeans. I pick up some of Eric's graduation cards he'd left on the dresser, idly wondering what to do with them. It doesn't seem quite right to throw them away.

Eric's bed has the comforter pulled back like he'd just crawled out from under it. I can almost see his 6-foot-4-inch frame on the bed, one lanky leg hanging over. And I can almost hear him speak. "Hey Mom—can you pray with me?" A childhood habit. A privilege. Sometimes a chore. Sometimes powerfully sacred. Confessions. Whispered worries about exams, girlfriends, school pressures. Dreams of future accomplishments.

That lump is there again. Tears come, surprising me. A memory flashes in my mind of Eric at 2—thick blond hair, blue eyes and deep dimples. I remember how he looked in a red turtleneck shirt and blue overalls, his chubby little arms around my neck.

"Look, Mom." Chris is pulling my arm. "I'm going to make this a study area over here. What do you think?"

"Great, Chris." I clumsily wipe away tears and try to smile in his direction. I don't want him to see me crying. He is so happy, and I feel so dismayed. I thought I had settled my problem with children leaving home two years earlier with Jon—in this very room. I had cried until my head hurt. Will every child's leaving cost this much?

Chris now has my full attention, like a long-awaited and loved guest who only has a brief stay. And he wants a study area. You bet, darlin'.

Later, the phone rings. It's Eric. His dad is on the bedroom extension and I'm in the kitchen, plying him with unimportant questions about what they're eating, and how they've fixed their beds. Eric gives great detail to salad bars, people he's met, what they wear. He reluctantly hands the phone to Jon, our college junior. "Hi," I greet him brightly. "What's happening there?"

"Oh, nothing much. Oh hi, Chad. Yeah, I'm about ready. No, it's just my folks. Sorry, Mom. What were you saying?" He was friendly but impatient to go. We chat briefly before we hang up and I go to the bedroom to find Bill. He puts his arms around me, smiling. "Looks like we're working ourselves out of a job," he says. His arms feel good to me. Comforting. We hold each other without saying anything, smiling wistful, gentle smiles. We had our babies, loved them, watched them grow and pretended that we owned them. Now make-believe is over, and they're leaving.

How do I mourn the loss of their childhood? There are no books or seminars about that. No Hallmark cards. It's a private, parent matter. You cry a little, sort the scrapbooks, and smile into the future.

There is very real pain in letting our children go—but we must. Erma Bombeck said it well: "When mothers talk about the depression of the empty nest, they're not mourning the passing of all those wet towels on the floor, or the music that numbs your teeth, or even the bottle of capless shampoo dribbling down the shower drain. They're upset because they've gone from supervisor of a child's life to a spectator. It's like being the vice president of the United States."[5]

Letting go is a release, but something powerful happens when we do it. We must let go in order to grab on to the next part of our lives. Letting go is a heart issue. In major changes of life, it's time to examine where our hearts are—what's most precious to us, what we secretly cherish, protect, nourish. It is where we are most vulnerable. When we can peel off the layers of all else and relinquish our hearts to God, he will indeed be the Lord under whose wings we take refuge.

And as we let go, we embrace the new place God has for us.

Prayer

Why is it, Lord, that so often in life, you put things in our hands—and then you call us to let go of them? I am seeing in the changes of life that they are not mine anyway! I release all that you have given me, and I am reminded that I am but a steward of my life: a steward of relationships, and ultimately, my children, my husband, my friends, my work. All is yours. In Christ's name I release them. Amen.

Mapping Your Next Step

Be honest about your losses. Talk these over with someone; let the tears flow. Journal your thoughts, your pain.

Allow God into that place of pain, and receive his comfort. Find Scriptures that minister to you. Read the Book of Ruth.

- How did Naomi and Ruth process their losses?
- In what ways can you relate to any of their actions and/or statements?

- What destructive emotions in your life keep you from growing to the next phase? Write them down; confess them to God and ask for his healing; then destroy the paper.
- Are you stuck in the good things of the past? Thank God for them, and see how creative you can be at weaving them into something useful for the present.
- What are some positive steps you can take to let go?
- What losses have you suffered that you've not taken time to grieve? What's your plan to address these? Take these three steps:

1. Prayerfully voice or write that you accept these things into your spirit.
2. Name these sufferings as investments for your future by examining what good things exist because of them.
3. Creatively turn those good things into gain. For each good thing that came at the end of your suffering, name at least three ideas on how to strengthen it for now, for the future.

10

The Big Picture

Rahab:
An Eye on the Eternal

That is happiness; to be dissolved into something complete and great.

Willa Cather

Besides being a creative entrepreneur, Rahab was beautiful and intelligent. True, she was a harlot, but she ran her inn so well that she developed a loyal clientele among the leadership of the city. Rahab used the assets she had, and her body was one of them. Since she was very young, she knew men were attracted to her. Because women usually were on the bottom rung of the ladder in her society, Rahab used men, as they used her, to grow more powerful and successful. Men trusted her; she knew how to keep a confidence to protect the influential men who frequented her place. Her comfortable and well-appointed house was strategically located up over the gap of the two walls of Jericho and offered beautiful views of the valley and beyond.[1]

There was something stirring in her, though. It had started a couple of years ago when men talked around her table at the inn. The big story was the massive emigration of the children of Israel, who were wending their way back to claim their God-given land. Rahab heard the amazing story of the Red Sea parting for them and how Pharaoh's army was drowned in the pursuit. There was talk of the defeat of the Amorites, whom the Israelites completely destroyed. To Rahab, there was something unusual and fascinating about these people on the march toward their city. While it was terrifying, she sensed something divine about it. Something big.

Early one evening, two strangers came in to ask for an evening meal and lodging. As Rahab sat down to talk with them, she realized who they were—spies from the Israelites, who were just beyond the Jordan River. *This is it*, she thought with a strange mixture of fear and excitement. Soon after they'd eaten, she took them to the top of her house, where she liked to sit and weave her linen. She had piles of flax up there ready to use, and she hid them under it. "There are too many ears around," she said. "Stay up here for the night."

Sure enough, someone had noticed the men at Rahab's establishment and reported them to the king of Jericho. That evening, the king's messengers knocked at her door with a decree: "Bring out the men who have come into your house. They are spies sent here to discover the best way to attack us." Rahab thought fast and said, "The men were here earlier, but I didn't know where they were from. They left the city at dusk, as the city gates were about to close, and I don't know where they went. If you hurry, you can probably catch up with them" (Josh. 2:3–5 NLT).

The king's men left quickly to find them, and Rahab went upstairs to the spies. "I know the LORD has given you this land," she told them. "We are all afraid of you. Everyone is living in terror. For we have heard how the LORD made a dry path for you through the Red Sea when you left Egypt. . . . No wonder our hearts have melted in fear! No one has the courage to fight after hearing such things. For the LORD your God is the supreme God of the heavens above and the earth below. Now swear to me by the LORD that you will be kind to me and my family since I have helped you. Give me some guarantee that when Jericho is conquered, you will let me live, along with my father and mother, my brothers and sisters, and all their families" (Josh. 2:9–13 NLT).

The men offered their own lives as a guarantee for her safety and told her to leave a scarlet rope hanging from the window as a sign to the Israelites when they reached the city. They told her to have all of her family members inside the house. If they were in the house, they would be safe, and no one would lay a hand on them. Rahab agreed to the terms.

Since Rahab's house was close to the city wall, she let them down by a rope through the window. Before they left, she advised them to escape to the hill country and hide there for three days, until the men who were looking for them returned. In the days that followed, the people of Jericho felt an almost unbearable tension, because they knew the Israelites were not far away. When Rahab heard they'd crossed the Jordan River, she insisted that her whole family come to her house, and they obeyed immediately, aware of the danger.

From Rahab's place on the wall, she and her family watched as the Israelites began a very strange procession. Armed guards went ahead of priests, who were carrying the ark of the covenant; behind them were more armed guards and then thousands of warriors. The priests blew their rams' horns as they marched completely around the city. They did it again the next day, and they repeated the process for six straight days. Then on the seventh day, they marched seven times around the wall; when they were finished, the people sent up a deafening, thunderous shout, and the walls of the city literally crumbled.

Rahab was mesmerized. The God of the Hebrews surely was the one true God! And she believed. The two spies who had been to her house suddenly showed up in the confusion and shouting, and they escorted Rahab and her family to a safe place near Israel's camp. Their commander, Joshua, had given orders to protect her.

Rahab married Salmon, and tradition has it that Salmon was one of the original spies she hid. She became the mother of Boaz, who married Ruth, who gave birth to Obed; he was the father of Jesse, who was the father of King David. Matthew 1:5 lists Rahab in the lineage of Jesus.

Rahab was able to grasp the big picture. As she observed what was going on around her, the truth convinced and captivated her. She not only believed it, she risked her very life on the God of Israel. She left her old life to begin a new one as a believer in the house of Israel. Rahab didn't let her past defeat her, and the writer of Hebrews held up her life as an example of faith in Hebrews' "Hall of Fame" (11:31).

What Can We Learn from Rahab?

Deep in our hearts, we all want to find and fulfill a purpose bigger than ourselves. Only such a larger purpose can inspire us to heights we could never reach on our own. For each of us, the real purpose is personal and passionate: to know what we are here to do, and why.

Os Guinness

When we women reach a significant crossroads, like Rahab, we've seen a lot. At this point in life, you most likely have had some successes as well as failures. If you're like me, you may look back and wonder, *How could I have said or done that?* You may see that sometimes life is not fair, that incompetence is rewarded. That people you've trusted have clay feet. It can be a time when you are tempted to take a long vacation. But that's exactly the time to see the big picture, to have vision for what can be, to believe that the best is yet to be for you. Having a big-picture mentality gives a woman staying power.

Get Past Your Past

One thing I do, forgetting those things which are behind and reaching forward to those things which are ahead, I press toward the goal for the prize of the upward call of God in Christ Jesus.

Philippians 3:13–14

Rahab used her gifts of creativity and leadership in hiding the spies. Because she had the courage to believe, God restored her, and she became an integral part of the children of Israel. She didn't let her past life as a harlot stop her from going on to a new life of righteousness and of making a difference. What Rahab was is not as important as what she became. God took the raw material of her life, and as she stepped into belief in him, he used her in a powerful way.

To go on to make a difference, we can't get stuck on the past. Have you ever made a major goof? I certainly have. One such experience involved writing a book. After working on a manuscript for a couple of years, I finally submitted it to my publisher. I was unprepared for the response. The book was not what they'd anticipated, and I could either withdraw it or do a major rewrite. Devastated, I withdrew my manuscript and shoved it in a drawer. I decided I was through with writing and speaking, and I even quit journaling for a while. I thought with some bitterness, *What is the point? I make myself vulnerable in my writing, and it's not understood or accepted as I hoped. I'm going to get a job as a hostess in a nice, pleasant restaurant!*

As I look back, I can see that painful experience taught me a lot. I needed to learn to listen to my editor. I needed to learn how to write books instead of articles (which I'd done for the previous fifteen years). What got me back on my feet was the big picture. I identified with Jeremiah: "Then I said, 'I will not make mention of Him, nor speak anymore in His name.' But His word was in my heart like a burning fire shut up in my bones; I was weary of holding it back, and I could not" (Jer. 20:9).

I picked up my writing and speaking again with a fresh determination to be honest with myself and with others, and to immerse myself in God's Word so I could better articulate the message. Failure need not diminish us, nor quench the message God intends for us to give. Indeed, it can refine our message. When we are defensive and blame others for our failures, it profits us nothing. When we are honest and repentant, we learn humility. And that's a good thing. It's been said that God can use people who have made enough mistakes to make them humble.

Success can trip us up too. Joseph Stowell says that we in our culture are obsessed with our own significance, which makes us vulnerable to sin. He said, "If I live my life to advance my own glory, then I cannot live my life to advance glory to God."[2] To make a difference in the Second Calling, we must see that we are building on a grand scheme that is bigger than our mistakes and failures, bigger than our successes. Triumph can be tricky. While it's a wonderful thing to have, if we've been blessed by it in a certain area, we may be stuck looking back on that time, longing for that time, or trying to make it happen again. All we have is today. The past is past.

Humility is nothing but the truth. "What have we got that we have not received?" asks St. Paul. If I have re-

173

ceived everything, what good have I of my own? If we are convinced of this, we will never raise our heads in pride. If you are humble, nothing will touch you, neither praise nor disgrace, because you know what you are. . . . Self-knowledge puts us on our knees, and it is very necessary for love. For knowledge of God gives love, and knowledge of self gives humility.

Mother Teresa, *The Love of Christ*[3]

See the Future

Rahab saw beyond the obvious fact that an intimidating people was approaching her city. She realized there was the "rest of the story." She recognized that a miraculous power was at work. There had to be a big plan, a God who was in control. And she believed.

What is the big picture? God made our world; he made us and has a plan for us. His plan is good! His Word is true. He is not willing that any should perish. We sin, but he redeems. We are to love one another as he loves us. We are not to judge each other but restore one another. It's not all about us—God can accomplish his will any way he wants to. And most of all, God is faithful!

The big picture is the big scheme—it's what we can know, what we can hang on to. Why is it important to see the big picture? Because details change. While details are important, if they are all we see, they can be a form of legalism. If we hold on too tightly to details—or style, or how things are done, insisting that they be done "my way or no way"—eventually God will tear them away from us.

Corrie ten Boom said, "Hold everything in your hands lightly—otherwise it hurts when God pries your fingers open."

Jill loved music and was very involved in her church choir, including its Easter and Christmas productions. When she and her family moved to a new area, she was

174

disappointed to find the new church didn't have a choir or do musical productions. The rest of her family loved the new church, though, so she went along with them. But she was not happy, and she did not feel that God was using her.

Jill finally decided to become a volunteer at a nursing home. The residents liked to sing hymns, so every week she led them in singing as she played the piano. She also became involved at her daughter's junior high as an accompanist for band students who were rehearsing for the music festival.

In using her musical gift this way, she discovered a new joy and purpose. When Jill was stuck in the details of how things used to be, she couldn't see how things could be. Later, she expressed gratitude that God nudged her out of the church walls. As she established relationships with various people in the nursing home, as well as with the junior high students, Jill understood that her music was really a vehicle of the message she was to carry—not the main event itself. Mary Stewart wrote this prayer: "Keep us, O Lord, from pettiness; let us be large in thought, in word, in deed."[4]

It's important, as the old saying goes, to keep the main thing the main thing. Seeing the big picture gives us perspective and vision for what's ahead. Proverbs 29:18 says, "Where there is no vision, the people perish" (KJV). Jesus said to look at the fields and to pray for more workers in the harvest. That's big-picture stuff. When we look at our own lives, at people around us, what do we see?

Simon the Pharisee had Jesus in his house for dinner, and a sinful woman came in and anointed Jesus' feet with perfume. Jesus asked him, "Simon, do you see this woman?" At the moment, Simon definitely missed the big picture. He saw a woman who was intruding on his dinner party, a woman with a bad reputation who was pouring an embarrassing display of worship on the feet of Jesus. Jesus saw her as a woman who had been forgiven much.

When we notice people, what do we see? What do we think when we see a prostitute, an abortion clinic, or street people panhandling? Are we disgusted? Or do we see people for whom Christ died? What about when we see a woman who seems to have it all together, and yet it's obvious she doesn't know Jesus? What is our response?

Shirley Swafford went as a young missionary with her husband and family to eastern Europe. One day in a market, Shirley watched in horror as a man stomped on an old woman who was trying to sell a few potatoes to make a bit of money. She found out later that certain men controlled the market area (in a mafia sense), and if a person wanted to sell merchandise there, he or she had to pay a fee. The poor old woman was unable to pay him, so he kicked her out, quite literally.

Shirley began to ask God what she could do. Through several miraculous answers to prayer, she eventually helped some local women start their own business: a beauty parlor. It thrived, and the women were able to make some income. They also had a back room where Shirley led Bible studies. Shirley not only saw the need, she took action.

What are the possibilities where you live? There are places everywhere for God to use our gifts and talents if we just have the courage to open our eyes. People are desperate for meaning, for purpose. Materialism and the relative values that saturate our culture strongly affect families. Older people need others to stop and listen. There are many disenfranchised people—those recently out of prison, or in prison. The mentally ill need care and understanding. There are needs in our own homes—our parents, relatives, husbands, children, and grandchildren need our love and prayers. The ministry of prayer is big-picture stuff! It's recognizing the importance of the eternal. Hudson Taylor, founder of the China Inland Mission, said, "There are three stages in the work of God: Impossible; Difficult; Done."[5]

Keep Your Eyes on Jesus

"We are called to Someone, not to Something."[6] We are not the answer to people's needs—Jesus is. But we can point the way to him. If we can give a clear picture of Jesus, his magnetism will draw people. "Jesus was outside the city in deserted places—and they came to him from every quarter" (see Mark 1:45).

Keeping my eyes on Jesus means asking, What would Jesus do in my situation? How can I see my world with his eyes? Am I living for him—is he my audience of significance? More than ever, we must listen to Jesus' words and we must study the Bible, asking, What is this saying to me? not How can I use this to straighten out somebody else? Keeping our eyes on Jesus means being willing to use our talents and gifts for him because we are his, not necessarily to enhance our own sense of self-worth.

This isn't a popular message. It's tempting to look at our gifts, our talents, our callings as things that elevate our sense of self-worth and give us a purpose. And of course, they do. Nothing is more rewarding than engaging and celebrating one's gifts. It is right. But as C. S. Lewis pointed out,

> The more we get what we now call "ourselves" out of the way and let Him take over, the more truly ourselves we become. The more I resist Him and try to live on my own, the more I become dominated by my own heredity and upbringing and surroundings and natural desires. In fact what I so proudly call "myself" becomes merely the meeting place for trains of events which I never started and which I cannot stop.[7]

Keeping my eyes on Jesus means to see others—and myself—as he does. That means rejecting the world's value system and recognizing my value as a unique person God has created for a unique purpose. It's to understand that my value is not in whether I wear a size six, look great in

177

shorts, wear the right clothing, or have the right address. God has something so much bigger and deeper for me—and for you.

Rick Warren, in his excellent book *The Purpose Driven Life,* writes, "The purpose of your life is far greater than your own personal fulfillment, your peace of mind, or even your happiness. It's far greater than your family, your career, or even your wildest dreams and ambitions. If you want to know why you were placed on this planet, you must begin with God. You were born by his purpose and for his purpose."[8]

Sometimes, in our desire to develop and use our talents and gifts, our focus can subtly shift to how using our gifts enhances us or makes us successful. But if we study the whole context of what Jesus is talking about, it's clear that all we are given is *for* something. It's for the big picture.

A Big Mission Is Bigger than One Person

How can we, like Rahab and Joshua and the spies, take the risk to step into a new land? It's been said that you can accomplish much if you don't care who gets the credit. The journey to Canaan was even bigger than Moses, as great a leader as he was, and he died before he reached the Jordan River. When it was finally time for the Israelites to cross over, Joshua took the leadership and went on, not threatened by Moses' previous success (or mistakes). A big mission calls us to build on the work of others who have preceded us. Joshua stepped into Moses' sandals and picked up where Moses left off. He didn't take the Israelites back through the wilderness to do it his way.

In 1969 Kay Arthur and her husband, Jack, returned from the mission field because Kay was ill. Jack became a manager for a Christian radio station, and Kay taught a Bible study every week in Atlanta, Georgia, to 250 women.

The class grew to 1,700 women, and when Kay finally left that group and moved to Chattanooga, Tennessee, she and Jack began Precept. It grew out of Kay's passion to help people learn how to study God's Word and apply it to their lives, to learn to study the Bible inductively, "precept upon precept." To accommodate the crowds, they remodeled a barn on property near their home.

Through the success of Precept, Kay and Jack have trained others—their efforts have multiplied. Now there are countless teachers all over the world, and the ministry operates out of beautiful facilities that are in constant use. Hundreds of thousands of men and women in the United States, and in more than eighty-five countries, have learned how to study the Bible through Precept. Only eternity will reveal how many lives Kay and Jack, and the many thousands of teachers of God's Word all over the world, have touched. It's time for us to ask, What am I doing in this Second Calling that will have staying power? How can I work with others so that the work will go forward and bear eternal fruit?

This is a time in life to be intentional. This may be the most influential and powerful period of our lives. You can go one of two ways: Either fully engage life here, or spend the next few years on a slow slide to complacency. Either see the big picture and live what you believe, or quietly lose your vision. Sometimes we let details slow us down, but don't give up! Oswald Chambers wrote, "Of course following Christ is difficult. All glorious things are nobly difficult!"[9]

Make a Commitment to Truth

God's truth will hold us. Psalm 91:4 says, "His truth shall be your shield and buckler." The question too many are asking today is, Does it work? We should be asking, Is it true? This "relevant truth" is prevalent in our society, even in our churches. We are so terribly afraid of being intolerant in our culture that truth gets lost. But it's important to ask the right questions.

Phillip E. Johnson, professor at U.C.-Berkeley and author of *The Right Questions*, says that because we evangelical Christians have gotten bogged down in the wrong questions, we end up being defensive and defeated by the secular science community. Instead of engaging such debates as evolution on the first few verses of Genesis, we should go directly to John 1, which is the heart of it all: "In the beginning was the Word" (v. 1 NIV). Either there is a grand design, a Creator behind all this creation, or we are just evolved matter. Much actual scientific evidence points to an intelligent design. That's big-picture stuff that we can teach our children to counteract some of what they are hearing. There are moral absolutes, parameters to life. Right and wrong do exist.

How essential it is for us to know truth and to do our best to say it to our generation in a way they will hear it. Josh McDowell paints an alarming scenario. He writes,

> Picture a youth-group Bible study. The adult group leader, who has just finished reading a Scripture passage, turns to a student and asks, "Alicia, what does this verse mean?"
> Alicia, a professed Christian from a good Christian home, pauses to reflect on the passage. "Well," she begins, after a few moments of careful consideration, "what this verse means to me is. . . ." Chances are, most of us wouldn't even detect the subtle shift in meaning reflected in Alicia's use of the words *to me*. But the importance of those two tiny words must not be underestimated. They are indicative of another dangerous condition that exists among today's Christian young people: Most of them are not looking to the biblical text for truth; they are actually looking within themselves. The majority of today's youth (70 percent) say there is no absolute moral truth.[10]

This is especially alarming when we realize our nation is under attack from people who are fueled by passionate belief. The 9/11 terrorists should give us a wake-up call. They were men who had a fierce faith in their radical religion, a fierce hatred against all Americans, and a goal to "kill the infidels" and bring our society down. And there are many more like them.

My husband and I recently had dinner with Attorney General John Ashcroft. We were discussing the challenges that face our nation, and what is essential. John Ashcroft said, "We have a formidable enemy. They are disciplined, patient, and committed." I asked him, "What can the average person do to combat terrorism in our culture?" He replied thoughtfully, "The best thing we can do is to invest in our young people."

Look at the People in Your Life

Rahab's first priority when she made her statement of faith in the God of Israel was to ensure safety for her family: her parents, her siblings, their mates, and their children. God places certain people in your life. What do you see? Let your imagination and vision soar as your life changes, and be flexible about what you perceive as possibilities and needs. Kierkegaard said, "A possibility is a hint from God."[11] See new opportunities within your own neighborhood and church. Several couples we know are sacrificing financially from their retirement funds in order to pay for their grandchildren's education at Christian schools. It is one way they are seeing the big picture and making a difference.

My mother-in-law was one of four young children. Her father was an alcoholic, and her mother had to work to help support the family. Times were difficult. But an older neighbor, Mrs. Cook, made herself available to the children. She did not just see four poor kids with an abusive drunk for a father and a working mother; she saw children with potential. She invited them over, gave them cookies, and told them Bible stories as she made bread. Betty, my mother-in-law, says she remembers Mrs. Cook singing as she kneaded, "Out of my bondage, sorrow and night, Jesus, I come, Jesus, I come; into Thy freedom, gladness and light, Jesus, I come to Thee."[12]

Mrs. Cook took them to Sunday school and introduced them to Jesus. All of those children became vibrant Christians. One became a pastor, one a missionary, and the others leaders in local churches. And they all established Christian families who are involved in ministry. Mrs. Cook saw kingdom possibilities in the kids next door—she saw the big picture!

When we plant God's Word, we never know where it will go. We do know that God's Word does not return unto him void. I'm not sure whether Mrs. Cook ever knew how much she influenced the lives of those little children . . . and their children . . . and their grandchildren. But someday in heaven, she will!

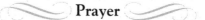

Prayer

Jesus, give me a discerning and willing heart to see the big picture. Give me courage to overcome my past mistakes; may I have persistence to pursue and to reach out, thoughtfully and purposefully. Help me to understand the dynamic of what it means to live and move in you. O God, may I be faithful to the journey you have called me to. Use me as you will! In Christ's name, amen.

Mapping Your Next Step

Read about Rahab in Joshua 2; 6:17–25; Hebrews 11:31; James 2:25. Also read the story of Jesus, the sinful woman, and Simon the Pharisee in Luke 7:36–50.

- In what ways did God use Rahab?
- What convinced her to believe?
- Why do you think Simon the Pharisee saw the woman the way he did?
- How did Jesus see her, and how can we see others the way he does?
- What are we creating or building that time cannot take away?
- What would you describe as being part of the big picture?

On the Anvil

Some people lie useless:
lives broken,
talents wasting,
fires quenched,
dreams dashed.
They are tossed in with the scrap iron, in desperate
need of repair, with no notion of purpose.
Others lie on the anvil:
hearts open,
hungry to change,
wounds healing,
visions clearing.
They welcome the painful pounding of the
blacksmith's hammer, longing to be
rebuilt, begging to be called.

Max Lucado[13]

11

My Place in the Big Picture

Esther:
Risk

I am only one, but still I am one.
I cannot do everything, but still I can do some-
    thing;
and because I cannot do everything, let me not
    refuse
to do something I can do.

Edward Everett Hale

Esther always had a strong sense of herself, even though her life had not been easy. She'd had to contend for it ever since both of her parents died when she was a young girl. Her wise and older cousin, Mordecai, adopted her and became the father figure she needed. They lived in Persia, since Nebuchadnezzar had brought their ancestors there when he defeated Jerusalem. The Jews gradually became an integral part of the region, and talented Mordecai rose to prominence and sat at the city gate, the center of commercial and legal activity.

Esther could never have imagined the extraordinary turn her life would take when a king's decree announced that she was one of the finalists in the search for a replacement for Queen Vashti. It was well known that Vashti had embarrassed King Xerxes by refusing to display herself at a national banquet for princes and nobles after days of feasting and drinking. It was not prudent to humiliate a king-sized ego, and Xerxes deposed Queen Vashti.

Esther had secretly applauded the queen for her courage, but to think she could be chosen as a possible replacement—surely that was a remote possibility! There were so many young virgins from whom the king could choose. Esther was taken to the palace with the other young women, where she caught the eye of Hegai, who was in charge of them. He immediately saw her potential and assigned seven servants to provide a special regimen of healthy food, beauty treatments, and training on how to please the king.

Mordecai missed her and dropped in occasionally to see her. Aware that the Jews had a strong enemy in the court—Haman—he warned her not to reveal her Jewish background. The day Esther was to go before the king, she glowed with health and beauty—but more than that, with an inner confidence. Her life was in God's hands.

As it turned out, the king was smitten by Esther and placed the royal crown on her head. What a celebration! The pronouncements, the appearances all became a blur as Esther began to comprehend that she was in the center of the most dominant political power of the region. She was queen! But she soon realized that this was not the romantic relationship she'd dreamed of as a little girl. It was instead a difficult and complex tightrope of power and intrigue.

Meanwhile, Mordecai was watching the power struggles from his own vantage point by the city gate. One day he went to Esther to urgently warn her of a plot he'd overheard from two of the king's officers to assassinate Xerxes. Esther reported it to the king, giving credit to Mordecai, and the two officers were hanged.

Haman was making his own power grab, and the king elevated him to a more influential position that required all to bow to him. When he went past Mordecai, on principle Mordecai did not bow. He could not bow to a man, only to his God. This infuriated Haman and triggered the old feelings of enmity for the Jews. He hated them. It would have been easy for him to have Mordecai killed, but instead, he hatched a more devastating plan. He convinced the king that the Jews were the enemy and persuaded him to make a decree throughout the land that every Jewish man, woman, and child be killed and their property confiscated.

Mordecai immediately told Esther, "You must do something. Go to the king." Esther knew the protocol: "You don't just walk in to the king uninvited. Those are immediate grounds to be killed, unless the king extends his scepter." Mordecai reminded her, "Esther, you are Jewish. You're not going to escape. Besides"—and he reminded her of her calling—"Who knows but that you have come to royal position for such a time as this?" (Esther 4:14 NIV).

She knew he was right. All the events of her life had to have been for something—and this was it. Esther took a deep breath. She remembered what happened when Queen Vashti stood up to the king. But she had to do what was right, regardless of the consequences. She told Mordecai to have all the Jews in the region fast and pray, and she and her maidens would as well. "If I perish, I perish," she said (Esther 4:16 NIV).

The king was glad to see her and extended his scepter, knowing she had a petition. But Esther was wise. She had a strategy. She invited the king and his top man, Haman, to a series of banquets. Gradually Esther revealed the truth: Haman was the enemy—out to destroy Esther and all her people; Mordecai was the king's friend, who had saved his life. The king had Haman hanged and elevated Mordecai to the second most powerful place in the land. A new decree was issued that allowed the Jews to fight for their lives, and Esther and her people were saved.

"Risk! Risk anything! Care no more for the opinion of others, for those voices. Do the hardest thing on earth for you. Act for yourself! Face the truth."[1]

What We Can Learn from Esther

Some Risks Are Worth Taking

Since we have such a hope, we are very bold.

2 Corinthians 3:12 NIV

Esther must have been afraid. But she knew if she did nothing, her people would lose their lives. She said, "If I perish, I perish." Esther knew that some risks were worth taking and was willing to lay her life down to do what was right.

What's our big risk? What hinders us from stepping out? Maybe it's fear of failure or of not knowing what to do. Maybe it's feeling intimidated by other women who seem to know more. The biggest risk some of us face are the voices within our selves that say, "You can't do that. Who do you think you are? You'd never make it. You're past your prime."

Discern Your Abilities and Where to Use Them

The bravest are surely those who have the clearest vision of what is before them, glory and danger alike, and yet notwithstanding go out to meet it.

Thucydides, 400 B.C.

Esther saw the big picture and risked her life to take her place in it. When we see the big picture and ask God to show us our calling in it, he will. There is something exceedingly precious about answering the call of God, regardless of where it may take us.

How do we know what our calling is? What we are passionate about is a clue. Rick Warren says, "What I am able to do, God wants me to do."[2] And we become good at what we are passionate about. Passion helps the creative process; it inspires hope and dreams and possibilities. When we are passionate about using our gifts and talents for the big picture, we won't have to worry about purpose—it will be a natural consequence.

Our challenge at this place is to discern and understand where we are to put our efforts—what will best use our talents—and to have the courage to follow through with a plan.

Offer All You Are

You should continue on as you were when God called you.

1 Corinthians 7:20 NLT

Esther realized her calling was not from her position, her possessions, her title, her gender. It's true that God used those things, but her calling was from who she was: a Hebrew woman who wanted to live a life of righteousness before God. God used what she offered him, but her purpose transcended those things. She didn't forget the roots of her faith, and she not only saw the big picture, she stepped into an opportunity there.

She could have simply sat back and enjoyed her royalty, ignoring the desperate needs of her people. Instead she set aside her own comfort to meet the challenge. John 13 includes a tender description of Jesus during the Passover; the Scripture says that Jesus, even knowing who he was, washed the disciples' feet (see John 13:1–5).

When we know who we are, like Jesus at the Last Supper, or like Esther in the royal court of Xerxes, we can take up the towel of a servant with grace and assurance. That is true effectiveness. Peter Drucker says, "Efficiency is doing things right. Effectiveness is doing the right things."[3]

You can believe that there is a place for you in the big picture. The best gift you have to offer is who and what you are.

Del and Linda Roberts were pastors of a church they started in the Denver area, and their work at the church was everything to them. When Del received the diagnosis that his cancer was terminal, Linda said, "I fell apart, though he remained calm. Throughout his illness, he said, 'This is a win-win deal for me. If God heals me, I win. If he takes me home, I win.'" Del entered the presence of the Lord on April 9, 2000, at age fifty-two, leaving behind Linda and her two sons. Linda said, "For those who miss him, as I do every day, it is important to remember that the duration of your life is not as important as the donation of it. It's not how long you live but how you live."

Linda wondered what to do next. The church was getting a new pastor, and it seemed awkward to stay there. She still felt called to pastor, even though she was alone. She began to consider church planting in Los Angeles. Why L.A.? She says, "Because the nations of the world are there, and my second mission is single adults, whom it seems the traditional church is not reaching." And so she actually did it—she moved to Los Angeles, and from knowing how she and Del had planted a church together, she did it this time alone, using a school to begin holding the services. Linda said, "The last three years have not been easy, but I am convinced there is no benefit in wanting things to be the way they used to be. God's purpose and plan are always ahead of us. His grace is sufficient."

The church is now well under way, and she is immersed in her deepened calling as a pastor. She had always been in a support role as copastor with Del, but now God has assigned her Second Calling, and she is serving him from who she is: a child of God who has experienced God's grace.

Prayer Wins the Battle

The universe belongs to him who will, who can, who knows how to pray.

Rowland P. Quilter

First things first! Esther knew the task ahead of her was enormous; she knew she needed prayer and rallied those around her for support. And she knew where her strength was: God was mightier than the awesome power of King Xerxes.

One night, after the banquet with Esther and Haman, the king couldn't sleep and asked a servant to read from records of his reign. He realized he had never rewarded Mordecai's help. Coincidence?

No. Esther had no idea how the situation would be resolved, but she had covered it in prayer. God is at work in ways we cannot imagine as we pray and fast for people and situations. What a relief to know we don't have to engineer or orchestrate anything. God is in control!

The challenges before us are great too. Lots of times, we wonder what we should do about a situation. Prayer (and fasting) is a place to begin. This signals our dependence on God, not on ourselves, to get direction.

My friend Bobbi Panter, a wonderful woman, has contended with multiple sclerosis for years and now is in a wheelchair. But she has not let that deter her from a powerful and effective ministry of prayer in the local church. She realizes that prayer is our real work—it's where the battle is won or lost. She helps schedule days of prayer as well as organizes prayer requests through e-mail. It is not exaggerating to say that her ministry touches thousands.

Face Opposition When It Comes

Why not go out on a limb? Isn't that where the fruit is?

Frank Scully

Esther received a figurative kick in the pants from Morde-cai, who reminded her who she was and urged her to step up to the opportunity. Sometimes we need to hear from someone else, "Go for it! You can do it." Sometimes we need to encourage ourselves. Jude says, "Beloved, building yourselves up on your most holy faith, praying in the Holy Spirit, keep yourselves in the love of God" (vv. 20–21).

There is a wonderful story about the first person ever to go over and survive Niagara Falls: Annie Taylor. She was a sixty-three-year-old former ballroom dancer and etiquette teacher of young women. Her job ended as times were changing, and she needed to do something to make an income. When she was a little girl, she'd visited the falls with her father, and the challenge of going over them in a barrel never left her. And she did it!

Although she received some initial recognition and pay for some of her lectures about her dramatic experience, eventually others exploited her story, and she ended up living a life of obscurity and poverty. She sold pictures of herself and her barrel at 60 percent off the regular price outside a hotel at the falls. Yet she knew who she was and what she'd done, and she encouraged herself by saying that the most significant applause she received from any person was from herself.[4]

This time of life, when we are discovering our Second Calling, requires courage—and for the follower of Christ, that means faith. Catherine Marshall writes,

When we see fear through Jesus' eyes, it is the acting out of our disbelief in the loving Fatherliness of God. By our fretting . . . we are really saying, "I don't believe in any God who can help me. . . ." Our Father never forgets the way we humans really are. . . . Therefore, in almost every example of God breaking into life on earth, the opening words are, "Fear not." . . . Our Father knows that, like small children, we need constant reassurances.[5]

We need faith to meet the opportunity that may present itself only once. As Shakespeare eloquently wrote, "There is a tide in the affairs of men which taken at the flood, leads on to fortune; omitted, all the voyages of their life, is bound in the shallows."

Live a Contagious Calling

Preach the gospel continuously. If necessary, use words.

Augustine

Esther conducted herself in such a manner that the king asked her three times, "What is your petition?" By the way she lived her life, she gained a hearing. Esther was wise. She held back, used discretion. Sometimes we are more effective when we say less. She patiently did her homework and used strategy and creativity in planning banquets. And she succeeded in getting the king's ear. Paul said, "I have become all things to all men so that by all possible means I might save some" (1 Cor. 9:22 NIV). We can so live that others will ask us, "What is the reason for your hope?" (see 1 Peter 3:15).

Esther was not perfect. She had doubts and fears. She had losses to overcome. She was in a racial minority that many hated. But she was willing to see her place in the big picture and take a risk. This life of risk—of faith—is not grim or joyless. The women I know who are stepping into their Second Calling are living a contagious faith. They can hardly wait to get up in the morning, they're having such a blast! The challenges can be great, but there's something thrilling about meeting challenges with God.

Char Pagett married very young—she was only seventeen, and her husband, Bob, only eighteen. She worked to help pay his way as he went through Bible college. When he graduated, she was by his side as he was a youth pastor, and then she helped him in his works as a district youth director. She supported Bob all the way with energy and enthusiasm, and they were always a great team.

The Pagetts had three small daughters when tragedy struck their family in Hawaii. Bob was preaching for a youth convention there when their three-month-old, Pammy, died suddenly and unexpectedly of SIDS.

Devastated, they went home and tried to go on. Char became very ill with asthma and lung infections and even had to leave her family to live in Arizona for a time to try to get better. Over time, with God's healing touch, she improved. Bob accepted a job as a pastor in Santa Cruz, California. Again Char was right beside him, expressing her boundless energy and creativity through music programs and outreaches. The church grew and thrived. Their two daughters grew up and finished college.

We were with Bob and Char on a trip to eastern Europe and the Soviet Union as communism was crumbling, and we were privileged to help give away copies of the Bible in modern Russian at the Moscow Book Fair. It was a moving experience to give what we so readily take for granted to the outstretched hands of people hungry for God's Word.

Bob and Char came home with fresh vision. Americans have so much, and much of the world is so needy. They resigned their church, took the love offering the congregation gave them, and invested it in a new ministry to network resources in the United States with needs in other nations—to give a "cup of cold water in Jesus' name." Char's organization and attention to detail helped Bob launch

Assist International. Char says she answered their phone, "Assist International" and laughs as she says, "The person on the other end couldn't know that we were operating out of our back bedroom!"

That was ten years ago. Now they have built offices and warehouses, and this last year, more than $13 million worth of highly technical medical equipment was placed in countries all over the world: China, Siberia, Africa, South America, Cuba, eastern Europe, and anywhere there were needs. Assist International has also built and arranged the support of a Romanian orphanage. Assist has a staff of seven, which stretches all of them to their limit.

Char does the work of two people as well as being a dedicated and fun-loving grandmother to her nine grandchildren. She and Bob just finished taking their three thirteen-year-old grandsons (two of them twins) on overseas missions trips. One of their goals is to inspire their grandchildren with the challenge of missions. I think it's significant that Char loves roller coasters—to her, the life of faith is an adventure, and she's having the time of her life. Her calling is truly contagious.

My twenty-something friend Adriel graduated from college and worked for two years to save money to travel around the world. As she traveled in Europe and Asia, she became captivated by the thought that she could become a missionary. She came home and went through discipleship training with Youth With a Mission. She is now training other young people to preach the gospel in Australia. Adriel saw the big picture and found her place in it.

What Is My Place in the Big Picture?

My nourishment comes from doing the will of God, who sent me, and from finishing his work.

John 4:34 NLT

194

What opportunity lies before you? Although there are big challenges to consider, sometimes we overlook smaller ones—and miss wonderful chances to affect those around us. God specializes in turning small, insignificant things into amazing demonstrations of his love: A baby born in a manger. A small boy's lunch.

Maybe the holy nudge you are getting is to do something entirely new, something that may seem crazy to others. God wants to use you to make a unique difference in the world that no one else can. There is no one else like you! Sometimes it takes a while to find out what you're all about. Actually, it's a lifetime journey of studying and learning. Ephesians 5:10 says, "Try to find out what is pleasing to the Lord" (NLT).

For the past several years, Barbara Olds has suffered from a rare, chronic, and painful condition. Instead of focusing on what she could not do anymore, she looked at what she could: sew. She'd collected many scraps of material over the years, so she put her creativity to work and began making rag dolls (and they are adorable!). She sends these to Metro Ministry in New York City to give to Sunday school children who are from very poor homes. She also helps organize the food bank through her local church. Instead of being limited, Barbara is living a very fruitful life.

What I love about God is that he starts where we are. He uses what we give him and grows us from there. Fear indicates a place for us to grow. I think back to when my children were young, and how afraid I was to stay home alone. Or to drive on the freeway or fly in an airplane. Or to speak in front of people! God took me where I was, step by fearful step, and as I obeyed, he has helped me grow past the fears.

Little Things

I come in the little things,
Saith the Lord:
Not borne on morning wings

195

Of majesty, but I have set My Feet
Amidst the delicate and bladed wheat
That springs triumphant in the furrowed sod.
There do I dwell, in weakness and in power;
Not broken or divided, Saith our God!

Evelyn Underhill, *Immanence*[6]

We're Fed by Fulfilling His Purpose

The righteous shall flourish like a palm tree,
He shall grow like a cedar in Lebanon.
Those who are planted in the house of the Lord
Shall flourish in the courts of our God.
They shall still bear fruit in old age;
They shall be fresh and flourishing.

Psalm 92:12–14

It's reassuring to read in the Bible how so many women's lives were centered around food.

There was the Shunamite woman who fed the prophet Elisha (2 Kings 4). Then of course the famous Proverbs 31 woman, who "brings her food from afar. She also rises while it is yet night, and provides food for her household" (vv. 14–15).

Then there's the wonderful illustration of Peter's mother-in-law, and how Jesus healed her when she had a fever. And what does she do as soon as she is healed? She "served them" (Mark 1:31).

My life is definitely centered around food! When I married Bill, I didn't have a clue how much I would need to know about the subject—especially as we went on to have four hungry, growing sons and one daughter. One day, when three of our sons were teenagers, it seemed I couldn't fill them up, no matter what I put out on the kitchen counter.

They each had a friend or two over as well, and I was almost at the point of tears.

What shall I do, I remembered thinking in desperation. *Start cutting up trees and branches for extra fiber?*

Somehow I managed to get them full that day. Actually, I like cooking for my family, especially when they're hungry. It makes me feel as if I am giving sustenance and strength to go on.

In chapter 1, I used the story from John 4 that tells the story of Jesus at the well in Sychar, Samaria. But here's the rest of the story: His disciples went on into the city to buy food while Jesus stayed behind to rest. When Jesus' disciples came back from the city, they brought him something to eat. But Jesus—and I have to believe that his eyes were bright with purpose and joy—said, "My food is to do what God wants! He is the one who sent me. . . . I am sending you" (vv. 34, 38 CEV).

We too are fed by living out his purpose for us. Last week I prayed with a young woman who had just been released from prison. I led her in prayer, and her countenance softened as she was filled with joy and hope in knowing Jesus. Later I realized that I too felt "fed." No matter where God has uniquely placed you, when you do his will, you are nourished and fulfilled beyond your wildest dreams.

The questions before us at this place in life are these:

What do I see as a risk worth taking?
How can I take my place in the big picture?
What are the right things for me to do?

Prayer

Lord, it does not matter how you use me—only use me. I offer my life, my all to share and speak your truth, your Word, whether through silent, intercessory

197

*prayer, ordinary acts of kindness, public speaking,
writing, service, or offering a listening ear. May I
first have a heart that stays near your heart, then a
willingness to respond, in whatever way you desire!
Amen!*

Mapping Your Next Step

Read the Book of Esther.

- As you read Esther's story, what facts about her life inspire you?
- What opportunity is before you? What keeps you from stepping into that place?
- How can you use your passion and your gifts to make a difference?
- What in your life right now can be explained only by the supernatural grace of God?
- Have you abandoned a dream that you now feel it is time to pursue?
- How does the dream fit with what you see as your place in the big picture?
- Often what keeps us from stepping out is fear. What principles from Esther's life can help you confront your own fears?
- Do you have an understanding or appreciation of what your calling is? If so, how can you be true to the person God has made you to be?

12

My Life, My Calling

Mary of Bethany: Love Poured Out

We make a living by what we get, but we make a life by what we give.

Winston Churchill

Mary was aware that something momentous was about to happen to Jesus, her beloved Lord. As she'd listened to him the past couple of years, she had a growing understanding that his life was going to be poured out.

She could not bear to think how that might happen; she only recognized that his days on earth were very few. But she also believed that his sacrifice would be for something enormous that had to do with his mission of becoming the way of redemption. He was God; she knew that. He had clearly identified himself to her sister Martha: "I am the resurrection and the life; . . . whoever lives and believes in me will never die" (John 11:25–26 NIV). And then he had literally called Lazarus, their dead brother, from the grave—back to life!

When Jesus went again to Bethany, a dinner was given in his honor. The table was crowded with people, including the recently resurrected Lazarus. As usual, Martha was in charge of the dinner, and she was serving a delicious meal. And as usual, Mary listened intently, her heart full of love for him. Jesus had done so much for her—he opened her eyes to real truth. He brought Lazarus back from the dead. And she saw how he loved people, especially children—how he loved blessing them, laughing with and holding them. He brought hope to the hopeless, healing to the sick.

But his words—oh, his words were like liquid fire that went to the heart, convicting, purifying. And he called her his friend! How could she show her love for him? Mary wanted to live his words so that she could help spread the Good News: Jesus was the Son of God, and knowing him would change anyone's life.

The meal progressed, and the conversation was stimulating and provocative. But Mary knew there was something she must do. She left quietly and went to her room. She went to a box on a shelf and opened it, drawing out a beautiful alabaster jar. She cradled the smooth white jar in her hands. Her father had given it to her years ago, and it was her most precious possession. It contained pure nard, a fragrant oil from India, and it was extremely expensive and rare. Once the seal was broken, the entire perfume had to be poured out—it wouldn't keep.

Mary went back to the dining area, and the men, reclining as usual around the table, were engrossed in their conversation. Without a word, she went to Jesus and broke the seal of the alabaster jar, tears welling in her eyes. It was right that she do this. She poured the oil out over Jesus and began to wipe his feet, using her long, dark hair.

The distinct fragrance filled the air, and conversation suddenly ceased. The men stared at her, and a few exchanged glances. Judas, one of Jesus' followers, was disgusted with Mary. "That perfume was worth a small fortune! It should have been sold and given to the poor," he said.

Jesus said, "Leave her alone. . . . You will always have the poor among you, and you can help them whenever you want to. But I will not be here with you much longer." Jesus continued, "She has done what she could and has anointed my body for burial ahead of time. I assure you, wherever the Good News is preached throughout the world, this woman's deed will be talked about in her memory" (Mark 14:6–8 NLT).

What We Can Learn from Mary of Bethany

Give What Is Most Precious

> When I survey the wondrous cross
> On which the Prince of Glory died,
> My richest gain I count but loss,
> And pour contempt on all my pride.
>
> Isaac Watts

I stood at the jewelry counter, waiting to make my purchase, as the woman next to me was picking out a graduation gift for her niece. "I think I'll get her a cross," she said as she fingered several of the necklaces the clerk put on the counter. "Oh, this one is really cute!" she exclaimed. She picked up one engraved with flowers. "I'll get this—she would love it!" I took a quick breath. The cross is many things, but "cute" it is not.

As she made the transaction, I remembered that I too have a cross that I wear on occasion and sometimes don't see past the ornament. And though often the cross is an

201

ornament, what it truly represents is love poured out. It is a symbol of Jesus' life, broken and spilled out for love of us, and if we are truly his followers, Jesus said we will be known by our love: "Just as I have loved you, you should love each other. Your love for one another will prove to the world that you are my disciples" (John 13:34–35 NLT). Love will be the symbol we wear.

When he calls us to come follow him, he calls us to be broken for love of him—so that his love shines through us. Those watching us don't always understand the life we believers lead, and their reaction may be like those around the table when Mary poured her perfume over Jesus—"What a waste!"

But it is not. It is real life, the essence of real fulfillment.

Our following Jesus can be like Peter's experience. Jesus first called Peter to follow him while Peter was fishing. Jesus convinced Peter that being a fisher of men would be a lot more fulfilling. And Peter left his nets to follow Jesus. This was Peter's First Calling.

Then the following became more difficult. Things fell apart when Judas—maybe sent over the edge by Mary's outrageous gift—went to the religious leaders and betrayed Jesus. Jesus was arrested in the garden, tortured, and later crucified. Peter, who had sworn he would protect and follow Jesus to the death, denied Jesus three times, and Scripture says that during this time, Peter "followed at a distance" (Luke 22:54 NIV). Who wouldn't? It's hard to follow closely when there's a cross involved.

After Jesus' death, Peter, depressed over his Lord's death and disgusted with his own betrayal, decided to go fishing. The scene was replayed as it occurred when Jesus first called Peter—again, no luck with the fish. Then the resurrected Jesus appeared on the seashore and again loaded his nets with fish, and Peter joyfully waded to shore for a reunion with his risen Lord. (Maybe Jesus understood Peter's "love language"—fish!) On the shore, Jesus asked Peter three times, "Do you love me?" Peter told him, "Yes!" Jesus' response then was "Feed my lambs. . . . Take care of my sheep. . . . Feed my sheep." This time, when Jesus called Peter, he threw out a challenge: "Follow me!" (John 21:15–17, 19 NIV). And this was Peter's Second Calling.

Then Peter asked, "What about John?" Maybe Peter was thinking, *Isn't John special! Sure, he's the disciple Jesus loves! John didn't abandon Jesus at the cross—he was the only disciple there. There's probably a different set of rules for him.* We may think, *Some followers of Christ really make a difference. But they have assets, abilities. They haven't gone through what I have. They haven't divorced or experienced failure. Then there's me.*

When Jesus asks us again, "Do you love me?" it is a personal calling. It does not matter what's happened in the past or how God is dealing with someone else. The question is, How do you respond now? The Second Calling is a calling of the heart. Jesus said, "If any of you wants to be my follower, you must put aside your selfish ambition, shoulder your cross daily, and follow me. If you try to keep your life for yourself, you will lose it. But if you give up your life for me, you will find true life. And how do you benefit if you gain the whole world but lose or forfeit your own soul in the process?" (Luke 9:23–25 NLT).

Mary's heart was so captivated by Jesus, she didn't care what others thought and broke open the alabaster jar of ointment.

When our hearts are captivated by him, we're not motivated by what others think. We realize our security in being his. To the outward observer, our lives may not look radically new, yet when we intentionally follow Jesus this way, we are confronted with the question, Do you love him enough to break open that which is most precious to you—your lives, your time—to be emptied out so that he can fill you and use you to love and nourish others?

It's Time to Bear Fruit

I am the vine, you are the branches. He who abides in
Me, and I in him, bears much fruit; for without Me you
can do nothing.

John 15:5

Last week Bill and I worked on our yard, putting in plants
and trimming branches. One of our plants is a ground cover
called Vinca—a vine that grows low to the ground and has
purple flowers. It's beautiful, but some of the plants were
growing very slowly and not filling in the spot I wanted
them to near my front door.

The woman in charge of the garden center in our town
is famous for having a green thumb and can make anything flourish. I asked her for advice, and she said, "If you
want to make those vines really grow, give them a haircut!
Trim the stems way back, and all the energy will go into
the root—and as a consequence, the vine will grow like
crazy."

Aha! A light went on in my head: Trim the stems, and
the energy will go to the root, which will make the whole
plant grow. Jesus said in John 15 that when we stay plugged
into the Vine—our Father God—we will bear fruit. And
we'll bear even more fruit when we are pruned, cut back.
People who make a difference for God in the world are
subject to pruning. What does this mean? It may be a
financial or career reversal. It may come in the form of a
health crisis. It may come through loss of a loved one. Or
maybe you're feeling sidelined, not sure where your place
is now. For a fresh harvest of fruit, we need seasonal pruning. In a time of pruning, we can be like Mary and open
ourselves wholly to him, offering up all we have and are
for his purposes.

What Christ calls us to is a life in him, not a series of
accomplishments, or an accumulation of property, or a

statement of financial worth. Answering his call is the most vital thing we can do.

Tend Sheep, Feed Lambs

You will find, as you look back upon your life, that the moments that stand out are the moments when you have done things for others.

Henry Drummond

One spring, when our children were small, I was helping with vacation Bible school. My friend Sue and I were responsible for recruiting volunteers. One afternoon at a committee meeting, Sue told me, "I called Pauline [a middle-aged woman] to see if she could help us one hour a day for five mornings, and she said, 'No, because that's when I water my garden.'" Sue was incredulous. "It wasn't an excuse! Pauline was serious."

Sue and I stared at each other, openmouthed. What planet did that woman inhabit? I could not conceive of such thinking. How could watering peas and beans be more important than teaching children about God? Now, twenty-five years later, I find myself in the unexpected place of understanding Pauline—maybe even being like her. What is at the heart of such thinking? It can be weariness or ill health. Perhaps it's just easier to fill time with hobbies or recreation. Or maybe it's the same kind of thinking that prompted Peter to go back to fishing after Jesus was arrested and executed. Although it's hard to admit, sometimes we who work with people can become cynical, thinking, *I did all that, and look what happened. It's easier to invest in inanimate objects or things that can't talk back.* Maybe that's why empty nesters get little dogs: They're cute, they don't break your heart, and they don't have souls to worry about.

205

Your Second Calling

The point is that midlife can be a tempting place to turn the needs off, to become more complacent. As we grow older, we know more. We've seen more. And while we may not be bitter, we can become more clever at avoiding God, avoiding people. If we are not in midlife, this is still true: Experience can make cynics of anyone.

It's easy to become busy with the mundane. I love being home with my piano and my flowers, watching the sun stream through the windows on my gleaming wood floor. It's comfortable to spend time with my husband and family and friends, read good books, be entertained by movies, go on a shopping trip, take long walks. I like to reflect and think. These things give me great pleasure, and surely they are gifts from God.

But let's be honest: When we are on the verge of a life change—of embracing a new calling—we can find ourselves feeling selfish and lazy. We find it easier to avoid risks in order to stay comfortable. And I'm keenly aware that in this business of following Jesus, there's a fine balance. At one time in my life, I worked so frenetically for Jesus that I became ill before I finally understood that it was by grace I was saved, not by works. That is why I am so convinced of the necessity of taking periodic Selah breaks—time to stop and think before going forward; time to absorb his love and grace in order to be fruitful.

Alan Nelson writes,

Maturity allows us the flexibility to wash feet, to carry a cross, to unleash sanctified anger, and to overturn tables. That is the embodiment of brokenness. Living out the faith. Your entire life becomes a paradox. A sort of reckless abandon comes over the attitude of a person with a tamed soul. This is not thrill-seeking irresponsibility found in the world. It is more of a sense that "I don't have to survive. I don't have to control my own destiny; He does. I don't have to call the shots; He does. I am not able to accomplish all

I need to accomplish; He is." We are more apt to respond as Esther did when God's people needed a clutch play to save the game: "And if I perish, I perish" (Esther 4:16). Our recklessness is a growing desire to do whatever God wants us to do, because we are not consumed with other tasks, like ego enhancement, reputation, preservation, and making something of ourselves.[1]

Give: A Natural Outpouring

Let love be your highest goal.

1 Corinthians 14:1 NLT

When I asked on my survey, "Who made a difference in your life?" the response was: mothers, fathers, aunts, teachers—in other words, key people in one's life. Each of us is a key person in someone's life, and it's time for us to make that difference. The most effective way to do that is simply to live the transformed life in front of them. We've said a lot—now it's time to live it, to teach by example, to take the risks that are worth taking, to mentor out of our own life experiences, whether we feel we've succeeded or not.

Paul wrote to Titus, "Older women must train the younger women to love their husbands and their children, to live wisely and be pure, to take care of their homes, to do good" (2:4–5 NLT).

Mentoring is a very real need. While experience is a powerful teacher, we can also learn much from those younger than we are. I find myself being mentored at times by my own daughters and daughters-in-law as I listen to their experiences and what their world is like. Mentoring is simply sharing with one another what we have; it's letting our experience become available to others.

My friend Cindy Johnson is experiencing the emptying nest, but she has always had a great rapport with teenagers.

Now she has an influential role working in the local high school. In our fractured and transient society, many young people are desperate to have someone see them and take time to hear them. Cindy does that, and she prays for them.

Another friend, Pat Markham, lives in British Columbia, and she is very gifted in hospitality and works in a restaurant. But more than that, she loves Jesus and has a club—a group of college-aged women with whom she meets regularly. She listens and talks to them about what's important in life. She has them come to her home and cooks for them. She has developed relationships with these young women, and they absolutely love her. She is able to speak into their lives about what it means to follow Jesus. The most effective mentoring occurs as a consequence of relationship.

Yesterday I received a wonderful gift in the mail, a bulky envelope, postmarked Montana. When I opened it, several letters spilled out with my mother's return address on them. They were letters she'd written in 1966 to a young man in my sister's class, who had been sent to Vietnam. Terry, now in his fifties and living in Montana, included a note, telling me that he had been sorting things from his army days and discovered the letters Mom had written. He thought I should have them.

She had sent him a newspaper clipping of my wedding, told him hometown news, like how the Conrad Cowboys' football team was doing against the other towns, and so on. But her most important message was to remind Terry over and over that God loved him and that he would be safe, no matter what happened, if he put his trust in God. She reassured him of her prayers. By the date and content of the letters, I began to put some things together: My mother was my age now when she wrote to Terry, a young man from home who was stationed in Vietnam.

At the time Mother started writing to him, she was experiencing the empty nest big-time—several of her children were leaving at once. My oldest sister was in the Philippines for a four-year missions assignment. My brother had just married and moved some distance away. My sister had taken a job in North Dakota. I had married Bill and moved to San Francisco.

Mom's children were her life, and she grieved as we left. But now that I see the whole scope of her life, I see that even more, Jesus was her life—and out of love for him, she noticed a young man far from home and wrote him letters of encouragement and prayer. Terry wrote to me, "As I read the letters, I remembered what a unique and priceless quality your mother was in God's service. She did not hold God's love as a personal possession that needed interpretation for others . . . but viewed God's love as matter of fact and the undisputed salvation of all. . . . I am sending these letters to you rather than discarding them with the hope that some of the things she said may afford you the opportunity to reflect again on her goodness."[2]

Terry is a follower of Christ today, and God did protect him during his Vietnam experience. As I read Mother's letters, I again heard her familiar voice and gentle, self-effacing humor smiling through the pages. I called my sisters to see if they had been aware of the correspondence, and none of them had. Leave it to my mother to write to a young man, a stranger, in the service and not even make a big deal of it! But a homesick and scared young man had read those letters and kept them for thirty-eight years. How many people did my mother influence? Countless folks, and I still hear from them occasionally.

After my father died, Mother moved to Oregon, and one of her neighbors was an older man who had been in business for years. He had a bad experience with someone in leadership at church and was very bitter about Christians and God. One day as he was going over his "wounds" (again), my mother stopped him, took both of his hands in hers, and looked intently into his face. "Frank," she said gently but with great compassion, "God loves you very much." He changed the subject, but tears came into his eyes.

The lives my mother touched and encouraged were many—but she did it naturally, as a consequence of her own life in God. In Mother's journal, she wrote one of her favorite quotes by an unknown author:

> If you have Beethoven in you, what music you could compose . . .
> If you have Shakespeare in you, what words you could write . . .
> But if you have Christ in you—what a life you can live!

Like Mary, who poured out her most precious possession, we can give only what is ours to give: our lives. To pour out our lives means to give our time to others and develop relationships with them. We must love one another. It's one of the last things Jesus told us to do.

This Is Your Time

> Cling to Him, for He is your life and the length of your days.
>
> Deuteronomy 30:20

Jesus told the men at the table that Mary's breaking the alabaster jar was a wholehearted demonstration of love that would be remembered always. I think the deep-down longing we have to make a difference is that very thing: We want to be remembered for something good. Scripture says, "These three remain: faith, hope and love" (1 Cor. 13:13 NIV).

What remains? Faith. Hope. Love. That means relationship with God, relationships with people. Not projects, programs, positions, power. But people.

I believe this kind of life means allowing for interruptions, taking time for the important rather than the urgent. It means looking beyond the obvious in the world around us, being aware that the person in front of us has an eternal destiny and that by our words and actions, we can influence that person. I believe it means seeing life as an adventure, asking God, "What is the exciting thing you have for me today—as well as the next twenty years?"

Now is the time to step into the most effective place in your life. It is time more than ever to put your trust in him for the next assignment, the Second Calling, to watch for unexpected opportunity, and when it comes, to take it. It's time to be intentional about the message you are projecting. It's time to have courage in order to take an honest inventory, to see what needs to go and what things need to be strengthened or added.

It's time to respect your physical needs and realize how necessary it is to have time-outs, to hear from God, to be rested and restored in order to have a new perspective. It's time to believe once more for the fulfillment of the delayed dreams and promises of your life. It's time to fall in love again—to believe that the next part of life really is the best!—and to have a sense of wonder once more about the world around you, and to reinvest in your marriage and important relationships.

It's time to have a fresh understanding of your calling, to have the courage to say no to some things in order to say a burning yes to risking steps of faith—to experience wonderful new adventures with God.

There are still inspiring books to be written, innovative businesses and ministries to be started, songs to be composed and sung, paintings to be created, visions to be realized, lives of integrity and faith yet to be lived, and poured-out lives to make a difference in the world. The paradox of the kingdom says that when we give away our lives for him, we gain much. In our weakness, he becomes strong.

This piece by an unknown woman describes how he can shine through our lives:

My Quilt

As I faced my Maker at the last judgment, I knelt before the Lord along with all the other souls. Before each of us lay our lives, shaped into squares of a quilt, in many piles. An angel sat before each of us, sewing our quilt squares together into tapestries.

But as my angel took each piece of cloth off the pile, I noticed how ragged and empty my squares were. They were filled with giant holes. Each square was labeled with a part of my life that had been difficult—the challenges and temptations I faced in everyday life. I saw hardships that I endured, which were the largest holes of all. I glanced around me. Nobody else had such squares. Other than a tiny hole here and there, the other tapestries were filled with rich color and the bright hues of worldly fortune. I gazed upon my own life and was disheartened.

My angel was sewing the ragged pieces of cloth together, threadbare and empty. She looked as if she were binding air.

Finally the time came when each life was to be displayed and held up to the light, the scrutiny of truth. The others rose, each holding up his or her tapestry. So full their lives had been. My angel looked upon me and nodded for me to rise. My gaze dropped to the ground in shame. I hadn't had all the earthly fortunes. I had love in my life, and laughter. But there had also been trials of illness, and death, and false accusations that took from me my world as I knew it. I had to start over many times. I often struggled with the temptation to quit, only somehow to muster the strength to pick up and begin again. I spent many nights on my knees in prayer, asking for help and guidance in my life. I had often been held up to ridicule, which I endured painfully, each time offering it to the Father in hopes that I would not melt within my skin beneath the critical gaze of those who unfairly judged me.

And now, I had to face the truth. My life was what it was, and I had to accept it for what it was.

I rose and slowly lifted the combined squares of my life to the light. An awe-filled gasp filled the air. I glanced around at the others, who stared at me with wide eyes. Then I looked upon the tapestry before me. Light flooded the many holes, creating an image—the face of Christ. Then our Lord stood before me, with warmth and love in his eyes. He said: "Every time you gave over your life and troubles to me, they became my life, my hardships, and my struggles. Each point of light in your life came when you stepped aside and let me shine through, until there was more of me than there was of you."

But we have this treasure in earthen vessels, that the excellence of the power may be of God and not of us. . . . For our light affliction, which is but for a moment, is working for us a far more exceeding and eternal weight of glory.

2 Corinthians 4:7, 17

Just Common, Ordinary Women, Used by God

Lupe Dobbs, her family shattered and her life destroyed by alcohol, dared to believe God. She kept believing him, got out of jail, finished three degrees, supported her family, and became pastor of a church.

June Curtis, blessed by family and heritage, believed that she could make a difference by investing in lives. And she does, by pouring out her life into people such as Lupe Dobbs.

Mrs. Cook—just a neighbor lady—saw four children next door who needed Jesus and let them into her life. She believed God could change their lives, and he did! Out of those four came four pastors, a Christian psychologist, two missionaries, one Christian publisher; and strong families centered in faith in Jesus.

Linda Johnson makes a difference as a friend, mother, and pastor's wife but also has an effective ministry as a home-health nurse, caring for sick people and bringing the healing touch of Jesus.

Shirley Swafford, just a bystander at a market in eastern Europe, saw a need and asked God what she could do. Because of her faith, she is empowering many women in eastern Europe to help themselves.

Linda Swearingen, involved in government, went to a women's outreach in the women's prison and God "arrested" her for his purposes. Now she has established a ministry that helps women fresh out of prison create productive lives.

These women have made and are making a difference —and you can do it too!

Prayer

Jesus, our hearts are filled with love and gratitude for all you are, all you have done for us. Like Mary, we pour out what is most precious to us—and that is our lives. May our priorities, our relationships, our choices, and our actions reflect your amazing love. In Christ's name we pray, amen.

Mapping Your Next Step

Read Mark 14:8–9; John 12:1–8; John 15; John 21. Then try to imagine yourself in Mary's place.

- What would cause her to do such a thing as break an alabaster jar and anoint Jesus?
- How might your life become more fruitful?
- Pruning must be done every season for an abundant harvest. Have you noticed different seasons of God's pruning in your life? What were the results?
- Using the illustration of Peter's conversation with Jesus at the seashore, how can you answer his call to follow him? How would following him translate into action?
- Discuss this statement: "Sometimes we fear the risks of moving on more than the risks of sitting still."
- How can we have faith and courage to move on?

Notes

Introduction

1. U.S. Dept. of Health and Human Services, 2002, 4women.gov/Time Capsule/Century/Century.

2. Judith Reichman, M.D., *I'm Not in the Mood* (New York: Quill William Morrow, 1998), 33.

3. U.S. Dept. of Health and Human Services, 2002, 4women.gov/Time Capsule/Century/Century.

4. Tony Warren, *What Does Selah Mean?* mountainretreatorg.net.

5. Christiane Northrup, M.D., *The Wisdom of Menopause*, 7.

6. Revival in Belfast; Hosanna music; produced by Paul Mills for PCM Productions, 1999, Integrity Inc.

Chapter 1

1. Quoted in Ken Gire, *The Work of His Hands* (Ann Arbor, Mich.: Servant, 2002), 131.

2. Vonette Zachary Bright, *In Search of Identity: A Deeper Walk* (Nashville: Thomas Nelson, 1994), 344.

3. Warren W. Wiersbe, *Prayer, Praise and Promises: A Daily Walk through the Psalms* (Grand Rapids: Baker, 1993).

4. Calvin Miller, *Walking with the Saints* (Nashville: Thomas Nelson, 1995), 15.

5. Dr. Richard Dobbins, *Invisible Imprint* (Sisters, OR: UMI Publishers, 2001), 17.

6. Laurie Beth Jones, *Power of Positive Prophecy* (New York: Hyperion, 1999), 74.

217

7. Os Guinness, *The Call* (Nashville: Word, 1998), 6.

8. Oswald Chambers, *My Utmost for His Highest* (Westwood, N.J.: Barbour, 1984, 100.

Chapter 2

1. Julia A. F. Carney, 1845.

2. Henry Drummond, *The Greatest Thing in the World: Three Famous Classics* (New Canaan, Conn.: Keats Publishing, 1973), 17.

3. M. Craig Barnes, *Hustling God* (Grand Rapids: Zondervan, 1999), 51.

4. Jim Collins, *Good to Great* (New York: HarperCollins, 2001), 36.

5. John Ortberg, *The Life You've Always Wanted* (Grand Rapids: Zondervan, 1997), 64.

6. Al Ries and Jack Trout, *The Twenty-two Immutable Laws of Marketing* (New York: HarperCollins, 1993), 18.

Chapter 3

1. Barbara deAngelis, *Real Moments* (New York: Dell Publishing, 1994), 8.

2. Donald O. Clifton and Paula Nelson, *Soar with Your Strengths* (New York: Bantam Doubleday, 1992), 44.

3. Rick Warren, *The Purpose Driven Life* (Grand Rapids: Zondervan, 2002), 243.

Chapter 4

1. Paul Tournier, *Creative Suffering* (San Francisco: HarperSanFrancisco, 1983).

2. Rob Gilbert, ed., *More of the Best of Bits and Pieces* (Fairfield, N.J.: Economics Press, 1997).

3. Po Branson, *What Shall I Do with My Life?* (New York: Random House, 2002), 58.

4. James Allen, *As a Man Thinketh*, in *Guideposts Treasury of Inspiration* (New York: Doubleday, 1980), 79.

5. David Seamands, *Living with Your Dreams* (Wheaton: Victor Books, 1990), 17.

Chapter 5

1. Frederick Buechner, *Listening to Your Life* (San Francisco: Harper San Francisco, 1992), 2.

2. Thomas à Kempis, quoted in *Treasure Chest* (San Francisco: Harper San Francisco, 1995), 18.

218

3. Adapted from Andrew Murray, *Waiting on God* (London: Nisbet & Co., 1895), 44.

Chapter 7

1. Phillip C. McGraw, Ph.D., *Self Matters* (New York: Simon & Schuster, 2001), 72.
2. Chambers, *My Utmost for His Highest*, 210.
3. Douglas Steere, *Gleanings* (Nashville: Upper Room Books, 1986), 51.
4. Paul Tournier, *Creative Suffering*, 49.
5. Poem used by permission.

Chapter 8

1. Dave and Claudia Arp, *The Second Half of Marriage* (Grand Rapids: Zondervan, 1996), 124.
2. Lois Davitz, *Living in Sync: Men and Women in Love* (New York: Bergh, 1986).
3. Henri F. Amiel, quoted in H. Norman Wright, ed., *Quiet Moments for Couples* (Eugene, Oreg.: Harvest House, 1995).
4. William and Nancie Carmichael, *Lord Bless This Marriage* (Wheaton: Tyndale House, 1999), 180.
5. Robert Hass and Stephen Mitchell, *Into the Garden: A Wedding Anthology* (San Francisco: Harper Perennial, 1993), xv.

Chapter 9

1. Hannah Ward and Jennifer Wild, comps., *Doubleday Christian Quotation Collection* (New York: Doubleday, 1998), 287.
2. *A Prairie Home Companion Pretty Good Joke Book* (Minneapolis: High Bridge Company, 2001), 93.
3. St. Francis De Sales, quoted in *Treasure Chest* (New York: HarperCollins, 1995), 120.
4. Paul Tournier, *A Place for You* (New York: Harper & Row Publishers, 1968), 136.
5. Erma Bombeck, *Motherhood: The Second Oldest Profession* (New York: McGraw-Hill, 1983), 64.

Chapter 10

1. "According to archaeological findings, there was a space of about twelve to fifteen feet between the two walls surrounding the city, and houses of sun-dried brick were built over the gap between the two walls, supported by timbers laid from one wall to the other. Rahab's house was in one of these

strategic points." Edith Deen, *All the Women of the Bible* (Edison, N.J.: Castle Books, 1955), 65.

2. Joseph Stowell, speech at the Christian Booksellers' Convention, 26 June 1994.

3. Mother Teresa of Calcutta, *The Love of Christ* (New York: Harper & Row, 1982), 113.

4. Ward and Wild, *Doubleday Christian Quotation Collection*, 221.

5. James Hudson Taylor, *Bartlett's Book of Quotations*, 194.

6. Guinness, *The Call*, 43.

7. C. S. Lewis, quoted in ibid., 25.

8. Rick Warren, *The Purpose Driven Life* (Grand Rapids: Zondervan, 2002), 17.

9. Chambers, *My Utmost for His Highest*, 90.

10. Josh McDowell and Bob Hostetler, *Beyond Belief to Conviction* (Wheaton: Tyndale House, 2002), 11.

11. Søren Kierkegaard, quoted in Ward and Wild, *Doubleday Christian Quotation Collection*, 177.

12. William T. Sleeper, "Jesus, I Come." Public domain.

13. Max Lucado, *On the Anvil* (Wheaton: Tyndale House, 1985), xvi.

Chapter 11

1. Katherine Mansfield, quoted in *Treasure Chest*, 79.

2. Warren, *Purpose Driven Life*, 242–43.

3. Peter Drucker, quoted in Bob Buford, *Halftime* (Grand Rapids: Zondervan, 1994), 82.

4. Joan Murray, *Queen of the Mist* (Boston: Beacon Press, 1999).

5. Catherine Marshall, *Something More* (Carmel, N.Y.: Guideposts, 1974), 256–57.

6. Evelyn Underhill, "Little Things," in *The Oxford Book of English Mystical Verse* (Oxford University Press, 1917).

Chapter 12

1. Alan E. Nelson, *Broken in the Right Place* (Nashville: Thomas Nelson, 1994), 170.

2. Letter used by permission.

Acknowledgments

To the women who shared their stories in this book, I offer my deepest thanks. I am inspired and encouraged by your lives of honesty, integrity, and love. You are truly making a difference in this world, and I hope you know that. And to my Tuesday morning study and prayer group—I couldn't have done this without your support. I love each one of you!

Jeanette Thomason of Baker Book House—thank you so much for believing in this book. You are one of the bright stars in my life, and your encouragement and friendship mean so much. Kelley Meyne and Holly Halverson—I am indebted to you too for your insightful and careful editing that has been essential in the formation of this book. And thanks most of all to my husband, Bill—my original editor, sounding board, life partner, soul mate—for being there every step of the way.

Nancie Carmichael

Nancie Carmichael, a popular women's conference speaker nationwide and in Canada, ministers side-by-side with her husband, Bill, in pastoral work, for marriage retreats and family workshops, and in writing and publishing.

She writes The Growing Eagle column in *Woman's Touch* magazine and is the author of eight books, coauthor of five books with her husband, Bill, and a contributor to several others like *A Bright Tomorrow* and *The Desert Experience*. She was editor and the popular "The Deeper Life" columnist at the heart of *Virtue* magazine and with Bill helped establish and start up some of the industry's largest periodicals for Good Family Magazines. She's won several Evangelical Press Association awards for magazine interviews with Christian thinkers and personalities and her columns on spiritual and personal growth. In 1999 she was awarded an honorary doctorate from Western Baptist College (on the same day that her youngest son Andy graduated).

She and Bill have five children—Jon, married to Brittni; Eric, married to Carly; Chris, married to Jami; Andy; and Amy—and three grandchildren (Will, Kendsy, and Cali).

She's the former founder and president of Virtue Live! Ministries to incarcerated women and has been involved in sponsoring and leading conferences for women in prison for more than seventeen years.

In her spare time she hikes the Cascade mountains in her backyard, where she also loves to pick huckleberries in summertime and bring them home to bake incredible pies. She and Bill live in a log home near Sisters, Oregon.

Her wish for those she encounters is to share from her own life as a wife, mother, and friend "the fact that we can trust God no matter what life throws at us." She says, "If I'm sure of anything, I know that he redeems and restores all that we place in his hands."

For speaking engagements, visit
www.nanciecarmichael.com